DANCING
WITH DADDY

BETSY PETERSEN

DANCING
WITH DADDY

A CHILDHOOD LOST AND A LIFE REGAINED

BANTAM BOOKS
NEW YORK • TORONTO • LONDON • SYDNEY • AUCKLAND

The author gratefully acknowledges permission to reproduce excerpts from letters written by Kitty Friesen, Bill Gallagher, Dr. John Ratcliffe, Dr. William Silen, Dr. Alex Weisskopf, and other friends, colleagues, and patients of her father; and to reproduce excerpts from the eulogy written by Gerald Egelston.

Dancing with Daddy
A Bantam Book / July 1991

Library of Congress Cataloging-in-Publication Data
Petersen, Betsy.
Dancing with Daddy : a childhood lost and a life regained / by
Betsy Petersen.
p. cm.
ISBN 0-553-07374-5
1. Petersen, Betsy. 2. Incest victims—United States—Biography.
3. Adult child sexual abuse victims—United States—Biography.
I. Title.
HQ72.U53P474   1991
362.7′6—dc20   90-21562
                                                        CIP

Published simultaneously in the United States and Canada

Bantam Books are published by Bantam Books, a division of Bantam
Doubleday Dell Publishing Group, Inc. Its trademark, consisting of the
words "Bantam Books" and the portrayal of a rooster, is Registered in U.S.
Patent and Trademark Office and in other countries. Marca Registrada.
Bantam Books, 666 Fifth Avenue, New York, New York 10103.

PRINTED IN THE UNITED STATES OF AMERICA

RRH   0 9 8 7 6 5 4 3 2 1

*This book is for my husband, Jim,
and our sons, William and Tom.*

THANK YOU

Patricia Browne, Val Gross, Erin Kelly, Linda Loewenthal, Ferrol Mennen, Denise Michelet, Kris O'Rourke, Patricia Kay Pace, Joyce Ann Pardue, Lynn Pearlmutter, Nessa Rapoport, Debra Reames, Julie Smith, Sophia Stone, Susan Tucker, Eric Vitiello, Donna Glee Williams, Chris Wiltz

CONTENTS

CONTENTS

DANCING
WITH DADDY

FAMILY PORTRAIT

In the picture there are shadows like ghosts on the wall behind us; those of my sister and my father are tall and powerful. My mother gazes at my father with a seductive smile. He meets her eyes. His smile is faint, almost not there. My sister Pat stands between them, looking out of the picture. I look out also as I sit, frowning, on my father's lap.

In the picture Pat is thirteen and I am two. It was taken in 1944, just before my father was sent to the Pacific; he often took pictures, or had them taken, to hold things still. He wears his uniform in the picture, and steel-rimmed army-issue glasses, and

1

his hands are huge next to my tiny ones, and slack. One hand holds my hip; the other brushes the inside of my thigh through my dress. I'm looking out of the picture in the same direction as my sister, and my face, like hers, is sad, puzzled, and angry. The anger is quite clear on my face; on my sister's face it is veiled. The three of us—my sister, my father, and I—face my mother in the picture; we are arrayed against her. My sister and I are her rivals, but she does not see that. We are invisible to her. She sees only my father.

KIDS: ONE

When I was pregnant with my first son I read all the books about nutrition and natural childbirth and breast-feeding, and planned how I would give my baby just what he needed. I had always done exactly what I was supposed to do, I reasoned, so why not this?

But my body betrayed me right from the start. My cervix wouldn't soften, my uterus wouldn't contract efficiently, and I labored ineffectually for most of the forty-four hours it took to deliver him.

And then, when I put him to my breast to nurse, he cried.

I nursed William for fourteen months, and each time he would take my nipple, suck for a few seconds, let go and cry, and then try again, and again, and again. He wasn't getting what he wanted, and I didn't know how to give it to him. And therefore, I thought, he didn't want me.

Now, thirteen years later, it seems obvious. My body tensed when he took my nipple in his mouth, and he felt it. I didn't feel it myself, because I was separating my consciousness from my body, just like I had as a child. I did not let myself hear the little girl's voice inside me crying: Let go of me, let go, leave me alone, I don't want you here, get away, GET AWAY, GET AWAY!

My younger son Tom did not pick up those signals; he nursed peacefully and endlessly. He would have nursed all day every day if I had let him, but I never let him have as much of me as he wanted. I remember him at the age of four or so, lying on the sofa, his arms outstretched, calling: "Give me . . . give me . . . give me . . . your *self.*" He never gave up, never stopped trying, and only after I began to remember what my father had done to me when I was a child did I see my resistance as a response not to my son, but to my father: I'm being used; I have to give him whatever he asks for, stop whatever I'm doing whenever he calls. The interruptions! Like a slap in the face: Don't take care of yourself, take care of me. He asks too much, he gets too close, he invades my space, my time, nothing is my own, it all belongs to him. He disintegrates me. Not my son. My father.

Until I was forty-five years old I did not know my father had molested me—yet that experience, so long repressed, kept me from being the mother I wanted to be, the mother I longed for when I was a child myself.

I have been acting out with my children the drama I learned at my mother's knee, and my father's: One, it seemed, wanted nothing to do with me, and the other wanted to gobble me up. I cast my children in those roles and taught them their lines.

Both my children woke up at night, every night, sometimes two or three times, from the time they were born until they were five or six years old. I used to compose myself for sleep and then startle awake, terrified, because I thought I heard them crying for me and I knew I would have to go and take care of them. I tried to believe it had something to do with nutrition: If I could just get them to drink a glass of milk at bedtime, everything would be fine. But they wouldn't.

I never thought of not going when they called, although their pediatrician told me to ignore their cries. I'm glad I ignored his advice, as it's clear to me now that they awoke at night because they weren't getting what they needed from me during the day. But I went because I didn't believe I could say no to them about anything. I saw my children the same way I saw my parents: huge and powerful, and at the same time intensely fragile. One wrong move from me and they would destroy me, or I them. I was afraid if I stopped them or foiled them in any way they would turn on me and eat me up, or else they would slide off the planet, out of reach, beyond my power to save them.

One day when they were ten and twelve years old they were fighting, just a normal fight between brothers, and all at once I couldn't stand it, could not stand it. I screamed, "EEEEEEEEE!" like a two-year-old. I clenched my fists and screwed up my eyes and then I threw myself down and gasped and sobbed and beat the floor. I was out of control. I thought I was going crazy. But when it was over I knew I had gone back to being a child for a little while. I was out of control because they were out of control. I had to make them stop fighting, but I couldn't. They wouldn't listen to me, they didn't care what I wanted, they didn't care how I felt, and I would be destroyed, caught in the middle and ground to bits. "They" were not my children but my parents.

William got down on the floor with me and held me in his arms and said softly, "It's okay. It's okay." I felt so ashamed of my tantrum, but so grateful for his comfort. I don't remember being held like that as a child; I didn't even know it was a possibility. But I also knew he needed to have a mommy, not to be one.

I had screamed like that once when he was little, about three. For some reason we were in the small bathroom behind the kitchen: tall narrow walls, barely enough room for the two of us. He did something, I don't remember what, and I got mad, furious. I screamed, and he touched my throat, took a fold of skin in his fingers, as if he were trying to turn off the scream. He must have thought it was his fault, and probably I thought so too.

I don't remember having tantrums as a child, but I was often told how I used to bite people. I was "the Neighborhood Terror." It said so in the family album, under a picture of me in braids and overalls, my fangs bared. Family History says I did it while my father was gone during the war, because that was such a bad time for our family; Family History says I stopped when he got back. But I remember biting somebody when I was in kindergarten, at least a year later. I remember my quick rage at the girl who wouldn't come when the teacher rang the bell. I remember the firm yet yielding texture of her knee as I sank my teeth into it.

For a while, for most of the year after Tom was born, William had four or five tantrums every day. I didn't tell anyone; I was too ashamed. Once he bit Tom and left tooth marks on his back; another time, riding in the car, I looked in the rearview mirror and saw him biting his own arm. Then one day he stopped. He stopped asking for what he wanted.

But Tom had tantrums, too, and he kept on and on, asking and asking and asking. He threw things on the floor and broke them, he turned over the furniture, he spit at me and cursed me. Pay attention, he was saying, the way my sister had: "She was always causing trouble," my mother said.

I didn't hear him asking. I didn't realize I was reliving my childhood, when the whole family was organized around my father's anger and our desperate need to appease him. I cast Tom in that role without knowing it.

If he'd done it in public I might have paid attention sooner, but in public he was charming, cooperative, attractive, well-mannered. His tantrums were a secret. Nobody outside the family knew about them, until finally one day I mentioned them in passing to the guidance counselor at his school, someone I respected and trusted. I was too embarrassed to tell her everything, but I told her a little bit, and she sent me to Kris, a wise, compassionate therapist who understood that the best way to help Tom was to help me.

Growing up in my family, I knew I had to eat my pain. Then my parents wouldn't have to see it. They wouldn't have to feel challenged to look inside themselves for the causes of my distress. This was the most important way I protected them. I try not to eat my pain now, but sometimes I still do. I eat my pain, my husband eats his pain, William eats his pain; but Tom dresses his up like anger and spits it out. He is our prophet, telling the truth we don't want to hear.

I had expected passive children who would mold themselves to me, as I molded myself to my parents, anticipating their wants, following just behind them, careful not to cross their line of sight. But my children wiggled, and cried, and demanded my attention. They did things I didn't want them to do and refused to do things I did want them to do, just like any child who's not too scared to take that risk.

I wanted to predict and control everything we did together. If I could stick to my agenda, I wouldn't be tossed about by their whims, like clothes in the Bendix washer where we lived when I was the Neighborhood Terror. But my children wouldn't march to my drum, so I was angry all the time. One day I took William to rent the video of *Space Balls* and he decided he wanted to get *Explorers* instead, and I got angry. "You don't have to get mad all the time," he said in a low voice, as if he were telling me a secret he didn't want anybody to hear. "Would you please not get so mad all the time?"

I remember how it felt to be on the receiving end of that quick rage: how it would all go bad in a moment. All I knew was that I had done something, and now my mother was turning away from me. It was like seeing the sun go out, being left alone in the fog and wind, uncovered, with no place to go to get warm. And I couldn't keep it from happening. My mother did it to me. And I did it to my children.

But I remember the night when I held William in the middle of the night and sang to him, tunes flowing through my mind and out of my mouth as they never had before. He was only a few weeks old, and I was so grateful to have him. I remember carrying him down the stairs on my hip when the doorbell rang, his bald head erect on his strong neck, his intellect blazing from blue eyes that took everything in, his palpable expectation that answering the door would be a great adventure. And I remember Tom's early smile, full of authentic merriment long before the time the books said he was supposed to be smiling. I remember him in midair, jumping off a motel diving board in his orange swim sweater, his arms outstretched and his mouth open to yell, for reasons known only to himself, *"Agua!"* My children are not my parents.

To know how much I love them is to know what I didn't give them, what they missed and what I missed. As I feel my love for them breaking out, the sadness I tried so hard not to feel breaks out with it. I use my hands to stuff the sobs back in, to eat the terrible grief, the knowledge that I missed the chance to give them what they needed then, when they were small. But if I want to be close to them, I have to let myself feel this pain, to cry for them and for me, because I spent their childhood as I spent my own, trying to protect myself.

My therapist said, "When you find yourself repeating those old patterns—" and I thought she was going to say something like, *that tells you how powerful they are,* but instead she said, "then you have a chance to change them."

My tears flowed like rain after a drought: I can get out of this desert, I can change the way I am with my children. We can be delivered from this body of death.

DOCTOR'S
DAUGHTER

When I was four my family moved from a fog-shrouded apartment near the ocean in San Francisco to a house down the Peninsula in Burlingame. When I woke up the first morning to see sun streaming through my window, it seemed as strange as snow.

But there was still fog sometimes. When I walked to school through it, I always expected to walk into the heart of it, into a place where I would be surrounded by mist, invisible. But instead it would recede and recede ahead of me until the big white school building came into view. By recess, when I went outside to play, the sun would be shining.

When I was growing up, the world outside—school, church, the houses of my friends—was a refuge. It was at home that I felt lost in mist. Yet I carried with me into the world a set of memories I called happy, from a childhood I called happy.

My father died when I was thirty-seven. I had not yet begun to remember what he did to me when I was a child, and would not for another eight years; I only knew I could not grieve. Trying to make myself have feelings, I took out my memories and shuffled through them like a pack of cards, a game of solitaire I played to make myself feel connected to him.

From the time I was four or five, my father used to take me with him to make hospital rounds on Sunday mornings. I saw the welcoming light in the nurses' eyes when he came down the hall, and assumed that they loved him as I did. I heard the respectful way they addressed him, and me. "Dr. Ervin's daughter!" That seemed to confer upon me an almost visible halo.

After rounds we'd go and look at the skeleton in the basement, which my father named Oswald, and my father would wiggle its jaw. Then he'd take me walking through the hospital garden, where there was a reflecting ball on a pedestal, and a bridge over the San Mateo Creek. A bay tree hung over the bridge, and he'd always pick one leaf and crush it and hold it under my nose for me to smell.

At home my mother would just be getting up, and he'd make her coffee and then fix a batch of pancakes. He cooked them three at a time, and I raced with him to see if I could finish eating them before the next three arrived on my plate.

If he wasn't on call he might take me bike riding. He'd ride on the outside, to protect me from the traffic. At Coyote Point he'd pick a eucalyptus leaf and hold it like the bay leaf for me to smell. He would tell me about the trees and shrubs we saw, and we'd walk on the gray, damp, gravelly sand of the beach.

Sometimes at night he would take me to get ice cream. We would walk up our street, Howard Avenue, and then turn left and walk along the railroad tracks to Borden's. Sometimes he would carry me on his shoulders for a little while, and I would get a glimpse of what the world looked like from his six-foot vantage point. Sometimes in Borden's we'd see one of his patients, who would smile at me with a face full of love for my father: "Your daddy's a wonderful man." When they asked me what I wanted to be when I grew up, I'd say, "A doctor."

"Oh, a doctor just like your daddy," they'd say, laughing gently. After someone told me girls couldn't grow up to be doctors, I started saying I wanted to be a nurse. I would be one of those women whose faces lit up when they saw my father coming down the wide, shiny hall.

Whenever I got a splinter in my finger he took it out. He'd sterilize a sewing needle with one of the matches he kept handy to light his cigars, and then he'd put on his magnifying glasses and hold my hand under the reading light by his chair, breathing heavily as he concentrated on gently working the splinter out. For a long time I thought you had to be a surgeon to take out a splinter.

He used to tell me stories about Gertie Gorilla, a bad little gorilla who was always getting her sister, the good little Betsy Gorilla, into trouble. He often talked about the stories he told to children while he sewed up their cuts, and about how they'd sit quietly and listen and never notice he was doing something that would have made them howl if some other doctor had done it. I grew up believing he was special, special among men because he was a doctor, and special among doctors because he

12

was kind, gentle, accessible, because he listened, because his voice was soft and respectful.

His office was a familiar place to me. My mother and I would stop by to say hello when we were out running errands, and when I got a cold my mother would bring me to the ear, nose, and throat department to get my sinuses suctioned out. My father's nurse would come down from surgery to do the procedure, as a special favor because I was Dr. Ervin's daughter. I'd lie on the examining table with my head hanging over the end, and she'd sit beside me while she operated the machine. Afterwards I would sit on a big throne and breathe penicillin mist.

That was my own official version of my childhood, a time when I was special because I was my father's daughter. But other memories undercut the pretty ones. By the time my father died I had come to see the ambiguity which had been there all along, contradictions which blocked my tears and made my heart feel like a lump of coal.

When I got measles or mumps, one of the pediatricians would make a house call, but if I was just a little bit sick my mother took me to the clinic. It was important to be considerate; doctors were busy and you couldn't waste their time. They were always nice to me, my father's colleagues, but I believed their smiles hid a secret contempt like my father's.

At home I saw his irritation at his patients. He would tell stories about neurotics—crocks, he called them—who expected him to listen endlessly to their stories. The phone would ring and everyone—my father, my mother, my sister, my sister's doctor husband—would chorus, "Oh, balls!" I shared the camaraderie of this ritual, even though I never used my father's favorite expletive; we were insiders, sharing an adversity that helped to define our special status. One Sunday afternoon there was a kid who got an arrow in his cheek—a stupid kid, it was clear, who got an arrow in his cheek just to ruin my father's Sunday. I said it to a friend, copying my father's disgust: "Some dumb kid got an arrow in his cheek." My father acted like the victim of his patients: They monopolized his time and didn't pay their bills. He didn't say they were all like that, but he never told stories about patients who were funny, or brave, or showed grace under pressure.

So many of my memories are of my father as a doctor. Even his legendary sloppiness at home—the area around his armchair was a wasteland of cigar ashes, socks, and piled-up surgery journals—was seen in the family as something that went with being a doctor. When he cooked he washed his hands constantly and left the crumpled paper towels on the counter, along with vegetable peelings and mixing bowls and dirty pots. Surgeons washed their hands a lot, my mother said, and he was used to having the nurses pick up after him in the operating room.

My father was gone a lot, taking care of his patients and going to meetings: hospital staff meetings, two surgical societies, the county medical society. Once he gave a talk on the radio: I remember his voice coming out of the big console in the living room while the dog barked madly.

When he went out in the evening my mother and I used to play cards. We had a paperback book of card games, and we'd try them out one after the other, all the two-handed ones. My mother used to talk about how she learned to play bridge from off-duty interns after she married my father, and the summer before I went to college she hired somebody to teach me to play, so that when I went away I would not be a neophyte at the mercy of such experts. She said she wanted to spare me the sarcasm and condescension she had endured at their hands.

Before I was born my mother had been a social worker with the welfare department in San Francisco. When I was growing up she was active in volunteer work, including the PTA at my schools. She was there when I got home from school. She drove car pools and made me write thank-you notes. When I went to college she decided to get a master's degree in social work at Berkeley, where she had done her undergraduate work. She became a psychiatric social worker and worked as a therapist for a number of years, and she went to workshops, at Esalen and elsewhere, with the leading lights of California psychotherapy, people like Fritz Perls and Virginia Satir. She was and is an intelligent, independent woman who loves music, reading, and travel. She has many friends: Some of them she has known since high school; some are my age or even younger.

Yet growing up I remember my mother almost exclusively as a satellite of my father. I remember her flattering my father, defending my father, interpreting my father, reacting to my father, obeying my father. He often told her, for instance, to leave the dishes after dinner, and especially after a party; on many Sunday mornings the house was permeated with the smell of stale wine, and the kitchen counters were littered with food-smeared plates, crusts of sourdough French bread, and crumpled paper towels.

Once, while my sister and her husband were living with us, my father complained that living with the three Ervin "women" (I was twelve) was like living with three panthers. I took him to mean that we were always yowling and carrying on; but perhaps he also meant to suggest a certain dangerous sensuality. My mother hired a dressmaker to make us each a pair of velvet "panther pants," which we wore at family parties for years. This, like our shared disgust for people who hurt themselves on weekends, was a source of camaraderie, something that set us apart from other families and defined us in terms of our center: my father.

My mother took me with her almost every day to run errands, to the laundry, the shoemaker, the gourmet market, where sometimes she'd buy me a little cake of pressed maple sugar. We went often to the post office, a huge, echoing hall with marble floors and counters, where once when she was mailing a package I said, with an eye on the man behind the counter, "Is that the one with the heroin in it?" She chided me for embarrassing her, but she told the story for years afterwards.

It was the sort of joke my father loved: It put people off balance and made them uncomfortable. One of his favorite stories concerned a friend whose dog used to relieve itself on the neighbor's lawn. The neighbor complained and complained. Finally, my father's friend, a pathologist who had some connections at the zoo, obtained what my father referred to as "an elephant turd," and left it on the neighbor's lawn.

My father loved sexual innuendoes and jokes. One of his favorites was about a woman who goes into a diner and asks for a ham sandwich. "I'm sorry, we're out of ham," says the counterman.

"Then give me a cheese sandwich," says the woman.

"We're out of cheese, too," says the counterman.

"Well, what *do* you have?"

"We have some very good tongue," says the counterman.

"Oh, no!" says the woman, outraged. "I could never eat something that came from an animal's mouth! Give me some eggs."

My father told me this joke whenever I refused to eat something he was offering me. He was an enthusiastic cook, with a taste for unusual combinations—water chestnuts in the gumbo, peanuts in the salad—and he liked strong-flavored foods, especially smelly cheeses. He used to boast that when I was a toddler

I would eat whatever he gave me. But as far back as I can remember I was suspicious of anything he offered. "Try it," he would wheedle. "It's good. You'll like it." But I knew better.

My father was heavy, like his mother. He often disparaged the greasy southern cooking of his childhood, and praised my mother's simple fare. But he wanted me to clean my plate and ask for seconds. "Come on, eat a little more," he'd say. "The cook's feelings will be hurt." I would feel guilty when he said this; but even though I was usually a compliant child, this was one thing he could not make me do.

My parents and my sister were casual about nudity. My parents slept in the nude and my sister and I would join them in bed on Sunday mornings to chat and clown around. I sometimes slept in the nude, too, because I thought they wanted me to, but I usually put some clothes on before I left my room. My sister walked around the house naked and sunbathed nude in the backyard. I felt ashamed of my own modesty, my wish to hide my body.

When I was around ten I went with my parents up to the Russian River to spend the weekend with friends. They lived in the woods, out of sight of the nearest house, and so, my parents told me, we would be able to sunbathe without bathing suits. We arrived, greeted our friends, and went inside to take off our clothes. I undressed as slowly as I could. Finally, I asked my mother, "Do I have to take everything off?"

"Of course not," she said, in a voice I'm sure she meant to be reassuring. "You can keep your panties on if you like." I spent the rest of the day sitting miserably on the deck in my underpants, trying not to look at the naked grownups.

My parents liked to say we could talk about anything in our family. When I was a teenager my friends used to drop in and sit around the dinner table, enjoying the way my parents treated them like adults. One night a male friend asked my father if a man was supposed to make sure his partner had an orgasm every time they made love.

I stared at the baked potato skin on my plate. My father laughed and replied, man-to-man, "You don't have to ring the bell every time." I kept my face impassive and managed somehow not to run from the table.

My friend actually used the word *orgasm*. It was not a word I ever heard either of my parents use. They never spoke so frankly to me, though I heard constant sexual references. They gave me no factual information about sex; nor did they make any attempt explicitly to transmit sexual values. I was allowed to read whatever I wanted from their large library, which included banned and once-banned books collected by my father—*Fanny Hill, Lady Chatterley's Lover, Lolita*—but reading was one thing, talking another. They told me to ask them if there was anything in the books I didn't understand. I never asked.

My father used to say my mother had a genius for putting her mark on a place. She could turn around twice, he said, shift something here, hang something there, and the place would be unmistakably hers. But when we moved to the suburbs we lived for ten years with the furniture that came with the house, the nondescript living room set, the awful maroon rug with its intricate, wearying patterns. Elsewhere in the house there were bare wood floors, and linoleum in the kitchen, and tile laid over the cement floor in the rumpus room. The Venetian blinds that came with the house still hung at the windows when we moved out, along with plain sheer curtains, turning gray. There was nothing soft.

My room had knotty pine walls, a dusty wood floor, a low, sagging bed covered with a pink jacquard spread, a little round maple table with two matching chairs, and a layer of mess everywhere. It seemed my mother—never my father—was always mad at me for being so sloppy. Once in a while I would come home from school to find she had tidied everything away, and I would relish the spareness of it until the mess took over again. I can't remember if she ever offered to help me clean it up, to show me what to do. When I grew up I learned to clean house as I learned so many other things, from a book.

She had help with the cleaning, a series of pleasant, energetic black women who came in once or twice a week. I did not know them well. Nevertheless, when our dog got run over, it was in Georgia's arms that I sobbed. I saw the wounded look on my mother's face, but for reasons I did not even try to understand, I believed she had no comfort to give me.

What people always noticed about our house was our books, which filled two bookcases on either side of the radio in the living room in Burlingame. By the time we moved to Hillsborough we had enough to fill a twenty-foot stretch of built-in shelves. "Have you really read all these books?" my friends would ask. We had pictures and artifacts, too: some watercolors, some pottery . . . nothing really valuable, but things that meant something to my parents. Later they filled the house with things from Mexico—tinwork from San Miguel de Allende, black pottery from Oaxaca, lacquerwork from Querétaro, a beautiful round table inlaid with turquoise tiles. My father, like all his partners, got a three-month sabbatical every few years, and we spent the spring of my seventh-grade year traveling in Mexico.

I didn't tell my mother until the day before we left how much I didn't want to go. I didn't want to leave the absorbing, intense social life of junior high school, and wished I could stay home with my sister and her husband, who would be living in our house while we were gone. But this possibility was never seriously discussed.

Before that trip my father bought me a journal bound in red leather with heavy cream-colored, gold-edged pages, and suggested I keep a record of our travels—the first expression of his wish for me to become a writer. But I found I could not live up to the challenge posed by the beautiful pages. After four days of dutiful, wooden entries—"We shopped all over town for some cigars for my father, but everyone thought we meant cigarettes, and then they told us to go someplace else"—I abandoned it. The last entry begins: "Los Alamos, Sonora, February 24, 1954," and then stops. That was the place where we visited the cemetery, walking around for hours, peering at the gravestones, while the conviction grew in me that death happened to everyone, and was going to happen to me. The terror of this realization stayed with me for many months, long after we returned to the States. Finally, one night as my mother and I were walking home from a friend's house after dark, I told her about my fears and asked her to send me to a psychiatrist so I could learn to deal with them.

"Oh, you don't need a psychiatrist," she said. "Everybody worries about dying."

In Mexico my father grew a beard—something that would have been frowned upon in the conservative clinic where he practiced—and was thrilled one night in Mazatlán, during Mardi Gras, when somebody pointed at him and called out, "Look! Hemingway!"

One night they left me in our room after dinner and went down to drink in the bar. When they came back they were quarreling. I pretended to be asleep until I couldn't stand it anymore and sat up in bed crying, "Stop it! Just stop it!" My mother came and sat on the edge of the bed and explained to me that all couples fought sometimes; it was nothing to worry about. Even when one person thought the other was an ass— she punctuated this part by glaring at my father—they still loved each other. I did not believe her.

All their friends had talked about what a wonderful opportunity this was for me, but my friends saw it as the disaster it was. I lived for mail from them. In Mexico City, where we stayed for a month, I comforted myself with ice cream. Every night after dinner in the hotel patio I would order a bowl of *helado de crema,* and then another, and very often a third. My father loved it—it was the one time in my life when I ate enough to please him. One night I announced that I planned to eat five bowls of ice cream, and did. My father took a picture of me sitting at the table under the umbrella with five empty metal pedestal bowls in front of me.

On the last night before we crossed the border we stayed in a motel owned by a man who had a son my age. The boy struck up a conversation with me in the restaurant and asked me if I would teach him to dance. With my parents' encouragement, I met him in the bar after dinner, but he said he was embarrassed to be seen by the men who were drinking there, and invited me to go to his room. I didn't want to go, but I didn't think it would be polite to say no. In his room, he turned on the radio, took me in his arms, and held me tightly against his chest. I could feel his heart beating. I looked in the mirror over his dresser and saw my own face looking back, and was instantly terrified. I ran away, back to the room I was sharing with my parents, and shut myself into the tiny alcove where my bed was. The boy followed, and knocked on the door. My parents came to my alcove and tried to get me to come out and talk to him but I refused, even though I understood that his feelings were hurt and it was my fault.

The next morning my father went into the bathroom and shaved off his beard and his moustache. He had grown the beard in Mexico, but he had worn a moustache for my whole life, except right after he came home from the war. When he came out of the bathroom in Mexico and I saw him clean-shaven, I ran back into my alcove and hid again.

My father wanted me to become a writer, and I did become a writer. In high school I showed him the drafts of all my papers, and he gave me advice. Mostly his advice consisted of two stories, repeated over and over. One of them was about the politician who counseled a younger colleague about public speaking: "First you tell 'em what you're gonna tell 'em, and then you tell 'em, and then you tell 'em what you told 'em." The other was about the farmer who advised his son to train a mule by hitting him in the face with a big stick: "First you have to get his undivided attention."

Writing was something I did to get my father's undivided attention. The first time I saw this clearly, when I was thirty, I quit writing. I told everyone I knew that I had retired. I went to a fabric store and stocked up on patterns and material, and went home and started sewing. I chose two soap operas for daily viewing—I think they were *Another World* and *General Hospital* —and whenever friends asked me what I was doing with myself, I told them I was sewing and watching the soaps. When I told my father, a puzzled frown spread across his face. "Are you gathering material for a novel?" he asked.

"I'm not writing anything anymore," I said.

"Why not?"

"Because I don't want to."

I hoped he got the point, though I lacked the courage to make it explicit. The point was that what he wanted me to be had nothing to do with what I was. But nine months later I was writing again, unable to abandon the work I loved even though he had chosen it for me.

I want to believe that my parents gave me nothing of value. When someone suggests that perhaps they did, I hear my voice growing loud and shrill: No. Nothing. Nothing!

LOOKING FOR
MOMMY

Sometimes it feels like the world is tilting and I'm sliding off, sliding off the planet into outer space: dark and cold, nothing to hold on to, nobody to hold on to me.

The fear is a physical feeling like nausea, rising up in my chest, mixing with the misery congealed there. I breathe high in my chest, shallow breaths, because on the exhale I sink down toward the fear and I'm afraid to sink too low.

Where is my mother? I look through all the rooms of my early childhood, all the places I can remember from when I was two and three and just four. She isn't there. In my memory she has gone: She was there, but now she's gone, and I don't know when or if she's coming back.

I remember a little candle I had in the shape of an angel, and the day it fell through the banister and broke on the floor below. I can feel the waxy texture of the head and body as I hold them, and the heat of my face as I sit there sobbing, tasting something ultimate and final for the first time. My babysitter sits beside me. "Your angel is in heaven with all the other angels," she says. I want my mommy, but she isn't here.

I remember arriving at nursery school, sitting on the toilet in a bathroom with an open door just off the entryway, then getting my temperature taken—the regular morning routine. I remember a big empty room, a shiny brown floor, a rocking horse, a big wooden box. The rocking horse is bigger than me. There are big windows at the end of the room, and outside it is cold and gray and the west wind blows in from the ocean. I smell apple juice and graham crackers and wet, salty air. But where is my mommy? It was a cooperative nursery school, she must have been there sometimes, but I can't find her. I want to sit on her lap until I'm ready to get down. I want to go off and ride the rocking horse when I'm ready, and find her there when I come back. But I can't find her.

I remember standing in the bathroom of our apartment in San Francisco. My mother is in her room, taking a nap. I am supposed to be taking a nap, too, but I have to go to the bathroom. Now I am staring at the gas heater next to the toilet. Flames glow behind a shiny metal grille. It looks like the stained-glass windows of the little houses we put under our Christmas tree. It looks warm and cozy inside where the flames are; something nice is happening there, but I can't imagine what it is. I'm outside. I want to get to the warmth and brightness, but I don't know how. I'm a giant, like Alice in Wonderland.

I'm too big to get in, but I can put something of mine inside and see what happens. I have a limp cotton apron, the kind an older child might make for her first sewing project. I push the tie through the hole toward the flame, letting it down into the heater until more and more of it is inside. . . . It catches on fire. I cry out, and my mother comes and grabs the burning apron and puts it in the basin. She is angry with me. She asks why I can never leave her alone to rest, why she must always be taking care of me.

I remember the laundry room in our apartment complex. I can see the row of front-loading Bendix washers with round glass windows through which I watch the clothes turning over and over while soapsuds are flung against the glass like surf. Just outside is a small play area, and in it a sandbox, small but deep —too deep to climb out of if you are three years old. I have been told that the deep sandbox keeps little children from running in the street while their mothers are putting clothes in the Bendix. I can feel the wet clammy sand, the rough cement sides of the sandbox; I can't see out, except for the gray sky. I can't get out. I have to wait for someone to come and get me. I have no memory of anyone coming.

I remember a family vacation at Clear Lake, a few months after I turned four. I can feel the sharp pebbles that hurt my feet on the beach, and see the writhing strip of live wasps and hornets at the waterline. I'm afraid to jump over them to get into the water. My sister, at fifteen as tall as a woman, steps across and leaves me behind. Later I am on the road that runs past the cabins. I am crying, and a man is asking me what cabin I came from. He takes me to the office: It is a cabin like the others, wooden walls with screen doors and windows, shaded by fir trees. They look in a big book and find where I belong. The man says I came all the way from Cabin 100 to Cabin 5, where he found me. I can't remember returning to my own cabin.

25

Later still I am in the car, alone in a dark parking lot. I am crying, and a strange woman is looking at me through the window. She opens the car door and picks me up and carries me into a room full of people and noise and music. I think my mother is angry with me for waking up. I remember her explanation: You have to be twenty-one to go into the place. My sister looks old enough, so she can go in with my parents, but I'm too little, so this night I have been put to bed in the car. I can remember the explanation, but I can't hear my mother's voice speaking the words, or see her face.

I can see my mother in my later childhood: driving the car as I sit beside her on the way to the laundry or the shoemaker's, standing at the sink, drinking and laughing at parties, yelling at my sister, reading to me from Grimm's *Fairy Tales* while I sit on the floor at her feet. But she is missing from almost every scene in those early years, even the ones I know she was part of.

I have access to my feelings in the present, the grief and terror, the sense of sliding off the planet into a cold, dark void where I will be utterly alone. And I have access to those pictures of the past, scenes in which my mother does not appear. But I cannot make the connection, cannot put the feelings into the scenes, experience once again what life was like for me then. Or am I afraid to? Yes. I am afraid to let go and sigh the deep sigh that might let me down into the emptiness of outer space.

DRUNKS

After we moved to the suburbs when I was four, friends of my parents would come down from the city on Saturdays, arriving in time for a late lunch. We would sit on the banquettes at the round kitchen table, eating pickles and nuts and smelly cheese and drinking beer. "Can I have a sip of beer?" I'd ask my father, and he'd say, "Get your little glass." My glass was a small cylinder—cheese spread had come in it—with a blue flower outlined on the side, and my father would pour an ounce of beer into it for me to drink. I can still taste the yeasty bubbles and see the clear amber topped with foam.

My father was fat, and he would stick his stomach out and mock himself. "Pretty soon I'll be so fat you won't be able to sit on my lap," he'd say, and I'd mark the air with my hand where his stomach, sometime in the future, would stick out so far it would make a shelf for me to sit on. "Your daddy's a dirty old man," he'd say, and the friends would laugh.

Sometimes the friends brought children with them, but usually I was the only child at the party. I sat with the grown-ups at the table, listening to the talk, laughing when they laughed, as the afternoon merged into evening and preparations for dinner began.

My parents had a friend I was taught to call "Uncle," who often joined the party. Once at the table he tried to kiss me, looking sad like an old dog. I smiled at him so he wouldn't get mad, and turned my head away, and the grown-ups laughed. My father told me later he was an alcoholic, and something called a "remittance man"—his relatives paid him to stay away.

They had another friend, also an alcoholic, a woman my mother always identified as someone from the days "when I was young and poor and lived on Telegraph Hill." One Saturday this woman and "Uncle" went down to the basement—we called it the "rumpus room"—and went to bed together. I didn't know about it at the time, but in later years I heard my father tell the story often. For him the best part was when he told how the sound rose straight up the heating duct to my sister's bedroom on the floor above. It was meant to be a funny story. My father laughed when he told it, and their friends laughed, and I laughed.

My mother changed when she drank, first her voice and then her face. Right away I could hear her tongue stumbling over consonants, as if she couldn't fit them all into her mouth.

And she laughed a lot. When she was sober her laugh was false: two notes, one in mid-range and one above, a Tinkerbell laugh, cute and phony as a glass ring from a gum machine.

But her drinking laugh sounded real. By midafternoon on those Saturdays her laugh, her voice, her face had become hectic, suffused with energy. She looked happy, alive, like her real self, the self she had chosen and wanted to be.

It was years before I realized that my father was getting drunk at those parties too. He just got quieter and quieter, and late in the evening he'd sit down on the floor with his back against the wall and go to sleep. "Daddy is being a mystic," my sister would say, quoting an empty-headed woman speaking to a drunk in a Peter Arno cartoon. I knew the cartoon, and I knew the man in the cartoon was drunk, but I didn't know my father was drunk. I thought he was sleepy because he worked so hard.

In the daytime, on weekdays, my mother was crabby and distracted. She would snap at me if I annoyed her, sometimes for no reason that I could see, although I believed it was my fault. Yet I often heard her say that I had been a good baby, was a good child; unlike my sister, I never caused any trouble. I took long naps; I went willingly to school; I kept quiet and asked no questions.

I was barely visible to her when she was sober. When she began to drink I disappeared, becoming like a ghost in a story who tries to communicate with the living but cannot make itself heard. Only once in a while when she was drinking would she seem to see me for a moment. She would peer at me, blinking owlishly, and then draw back and laugh, responding to my distress as if it were disapproval, and mocking it. I saw myself through her eyes as the strait-laced, dull bourgeoise, a foil for her glamor and vitality.

Very occasionally on a weekend there was no party at home, and no invitation to go out. When there was no company, only me to hear them, my parents drank and quarreled. One evening when I was eleven or so, I heard them starting up and resolved to stop them. I dressed up in funny clothes and painted my face, interrupting them over and over so they could applaud each new variation of my costume. In the pictures of me my father took that night, I look pretty, flushed with energy; I felt desperate panic.

My father was famous for the strong drinks he mixed for his guests, and once I was there when he put liquor in a drink he mixed for a woman who had reminded him several times that alcohol made her sick. It was his habit at parties—part of his philosophy of life—to mix the first few drinks extra strong, because that helped the party "take off."

When I was in college I asked him for some Dexedrine to help me study. That was the kind of relationship we had in the story we told ourselves: open, adult, up front about everything. He opened the cabinet in his bathroom and took out a quart bottle full of green tablets. "I got these for Joe," he told me. Joe was a close friend; my father was carrying on a flirtation with his wife. "Joe is an alcoholic," he told me, his voice full of self-importance, the family doctor who can be trusted to tell you the truth. "Sometimes Dexedrine is helpful for that." He doled out some green tablets. "I know you'll be careful with these," he said.

He had a story about Dexedrine. When it first became available it was manufactured as a syrup, and my father got a bottle of it and put some in the punch at a party. "That party really took off!" he said, with that chortle he had when he'd played a good joke on somebody.

One evening when I was five or six my parents took me with them to spend the evening with some friends. I suppose they couldn't find a babysitter, and my sister, who dated every weekend, rarely stayed with me. The friends' children, younger than I, had gone to sleep in their own beds, but I lingered on with the grown-ups, as was my habit at my parents' parties. The husband was in the kitchen with my mother—I could hear them talking in loud voices and laughing. The wife sat on my father's lap in a big easy chair. She lay across the arms of the chair, and he held her loosely, one hand on her thigh. She wore a thin black dress. She had a cloud of wavy black hair and deep, dark eyes, and an ample body. My father looked at her with a foolish smile, his eyes unfocused like the "mystic" in the Peter Arno cartoon, and I sat across the room from them and cried. "Don't you want to go upstairs and lie down?" asked the husband, hearing my sobs. But I wouldn't go. Maybe I was afraid of what my father and the wife might do if I left them alone. I sat on the sofa and cried until my parents took me home.

I saw my father look at my mother that way once, when I was eleven or twelve. They had some grapes they were going to make into wine, and my mother was going to squeeze the juice out of them with her feet. She wore a T-shirt of my father's tied between her legs, and a bandana around her head, as she stepped into the ten-gallon crock. Her voice was high-pitched and slurred, and my father's face looked blurred as he smiled at her with soft, loose lips. It should have been something private for the two of them, but they wanted me to be their witness. I sat on the hard basement steps and played my flute, because they wanted me to. I pretended to have fun, because they wanted me to; but I was very, very tired.

My parents drank beer in the afternoons, cocktails before dinner, and wine with dinner and afterwards. They drank jug wine that came in wicker-covered bottles, and poured it into little dark-blue glasses they'd bought on Olvera Street in Los Angeles soon after they were married. After dinner they would pile the dirty dishes haphazardly on the kitchen counter and move to the living room, where they would drink glass after

31

glass after glass of wine. If there were guests, there was conversation, which I was taught to consider brilliant and sophisticated. My mother would be in constant motion. Years later my father wrote, "To me she was a completely new species, sometimes gay, sometimes deeply serious; frivolous, fun-loving; sometimes giving with abandon, sometimes demanding imperiously; flitting from one mood to another with such dazzling speed that she blended them all." I remember her party self, her triangular smile, the upper corners drawn up toward the eyes, and the way one eye seemed lower than the other, not in the same latitude. The face of a stranger, not my mother. Her real face.

After everyone else had gone home, one other couple would remain. Usually there was a couple of the moment, somebody my parents were spending most of their free time with. These tandem romances usually lasted a year or two before my parents took up with someone new. My mother and the other man would laugh raucously while my father murmured softly in the woman's ear. My mother would reach out for the bottle of wine and very deliberately pour some into her glass, and then she would set it down very carefully; but in spite of her care it would clunk as it came down to meet the table a little sooner than she expected.

By this time her face would have gone soft, like butter in midsummer. She would peer at her companion in the candlelight, her eyes slitted, her lips soft and moist, pausing before she made another point in the deep conversation they were having. Sometimes she would verbally advance on her foe, trying to corner him. Sometimes she would roll her eyes and purse her lips and look deeply sad, as if to suggest that though she had known grief in her time, she was brave and gallant; nobody knew the trouble she'd seen.

I never knew how these conversations ended, because at some point my mother would ask, offhandedly, if I wanted to go to bed now. In case it was what they wanted, in case it made a difference what I did, I went.

One night when I was in high school I came home and saw my mother dancing around and around on the cork tile floor, swooping and laughing, while my father and their guest, a man I didn't know, egged her on. It was the worst—to me the worst—I'd ever seen her. I hated it, hated her. I pressed my lips together in a thin, disapproving line and spoke of other things in short, clipped sentences, the way we did in our family when we were angry. The next morning my father drove me to school, and in the car I said, my heart pounding, "Mother was really drunk last night." I had never in my life said aloud that either of them got drunk.

"She was fine until you came home," my father said. "She was happy, she was having a good time, and then you came home and made her feel bad."

"I'm afraid she's an alcoholic," I said.

"She's not an alcoholic," he said, his voice irritated, as if he were swatting a fly. He might have been saying: Get away from me. I have enough to take care of, earning enough money to buy your clothes; it isn't fair that I should have to be bothered with this too.

Loud silence lasted until we arrived at school. I fumbled with the door handle. "Open the door, asshole!" he snarled—the only time he ever called me anything worse than "knothead."

"Don't you call me names!" I shouted. "Don't you ever call me names!" I got out and slammed the door. That night he apologized for calling me "asshole," the only time he ever told me he was sorry for anything. He didn't mention my fears about my mother, then or ever.

I didn't talk about drinking again to either of my parents

until thirty years later, after my father died. Over lunch in a restaurant my mother said, "You're awfully quiet."

"I want to ask you something." I paused, and there was silence between us for a few moments. "Did you ever think Daddy might have a drinking problem?"

"I only saw him out of control three times," she answered. "Three times in forty years." Her voice was clear and strong, adult to adult. "He told me once that he appreciated my willingness to drink with him. . . . Why are you asking? Are you concerned your boys might have inherited something?"

"No. I'm asking because your drinking, yours and Daddy's, was a problem for me."

"It must have been awful," she said in her strong adult voice.

"Yes," I said. "It was."

She did not ask me to tell her just how awful it was.

In the thirty-seven years I knew him, I saw my father "out of control" many more times than three, if you consider crossed eyes, a shit-eating grin, mumbling speech, and a stumbling gait "out of control." One night when I was home from college on vacation, I heard his voice from their bedroom, so shrill it was almost falsetto, yelling at my mother: "Leave me alone! Leave me alone! Leave me alone!" I went in and talked to them and felt pleased afterwards that I had helped them to settle down. But the next night I heard him again: "Leave me alone! Leave me alone!" I did nothing.

At Thanksgiving and Christmas and other occasions when the extended family gathered, my father made strong drinks for everyone. Maybe it got worse as I got older; maybe I just noticed it more. I remember the last party we had before my sister died, when I was twenty-two. We sat around a plate-glass table set with sterling silver and platinum-rimmed china. It was my sister's house, and her husband's, but it was my father who made sure everyone got more than enough to drink. As everyone got drunker and drunker—one relative had to rush from the table at one point—we looked through the glass table at our feet on the floor below, and pretended we were in the *Ozzie and Harriet* show. After dinner my father murmured obscene Spanish words—the only Spanish words he knew—to my sister's house-keeper, a middle-aged Mexican Catholic.

At another party, several years after my sister died, the family gathered at my parents' cottage in the mountains. I was needlepointing a peace symbol for them—this was 1970, and they identified themselves with the peace movement and the young radicals of the time. My mother was drinking. Her face seemed to have fallen in on itself, a vortex of emotions. As I pushed my needle through the canvas, my mother, the Esalen veteran, said, "I feel you're trying to keep yourself aloof from us."

It was against the rules in our family for anyone to talk about what was really happening, so I did not say "I don't want to be close to you when you're drunk." Instead I answered, "I just like doing needlepoint," while inside I screamed: I hate you I hate you I hate you!

That night I dreamed my mother had a knife and was carving me into pieces, and I had a knife and was carving her into pieces. I woke at dawn, a thrill of terror running through me, and ran out of the house and down the trail to the water-fall. I stood panting beside it, staring into the clear running water and gulping deep breaths of the redwood-scented air as I struggled without hope to escape from my prison of pain and rage.

SISTERS

My first memory of her is standing in the big circle for "colors"—the lowering of the flag —at the army base. Just a vague sense of her next to me, tall and solemn like all the other tall and solemn people.

She was thirteen and I was two. It was during World War II, and we were living at the Presidio in San Francisco, where my father was stationed before he was sent to the Pacific.

She had a soldier boyfriend there, Private Fargo, somebody she used to meet at the base movies and walk home with. She didn't hide his existence from my parents, but she didn't tell them either. My father found out, and let Fargo know that a word to his commanding officer would have him transferred out in hours. Then my father let the romance continue. He taught me a little comedy routine: "What does the doggie say?" he would ask.

"Bow wow!" I would answer.

"And what does the kitty say?"

"Meow meow!"

"And what does Fargo say?"

"Arf arf!" I would say, finishing triumphantly, "Fargo is a wolf!".

My father took pictures of my sister outside that house, posed in a bathing suit and in one of his shirts that hung down to her thighs, suggesting she was naked underneath. In some of the pictures she is pouting, in some smiling. In all of them she looks beautiful and sexy, and much older than thirteen.

In the pictures my father took, her smile is bittersweet. In person she looked all sweet, but the camera saw the bitterness, and I saw it in the pictures. I noticed it when I was very young. I used to wonder about it and wish for her to be happy.

She was not my father's daughter, though I did not know this until years later. My mother married young, divorced soon, and went home—not to her mother, who had died when she was six, but to her grandmother.

Grandma had raised my mother, and Grandma raised my sister while my mother went to college, moved across the bay to San Francisco, and went to work. My mother saw my sister on weekends, but during the week my sister lived with the same family my mother had: Grandma, Grandpa, Great-Grandma, Aunt Gertrude, and Uncle Julius. My mother married my father when my sister was four; she went to live with them when she was eight.

When she was thirteen and I was two, my father went

overseas, and we moved to a garden apartment near the ocean. He came home nine months later. He came in the front door of our apartment wearing his army uniform, his face smooth and round without the moustache he had worn before he went away.

"Papa!" I yelled.

"You call him *that?*" my sister asked scornfully.

"What do you call him?" I asked, my face burning with embarrassment at my faux pas.

"Daddy!" she said, as if it should be obvious to anyone with any sense.

Yet he had taught her, I learned years later, to call him "Papa"—to distinguish him from her natural father, whom she called "Daddy"—and neither of us had ever called him anything else.

What magic did she hope to work by changing her name for my father? Did she mean to send him a message? "I want you to be a real daddy to me now. I don't want to do the things we did before you went away." Was that what she wanted to tell him? If so, he didn't get the message, or he chose to ignore it.

I remember her in the courtyard outside our apartment, sitting in a group of teenagers, drinking something ice-cold and black and fizzy out of a tall glass. "Can I have a sip?" I asked. She offered me the glass. I sipped. I thought it was the best drink I had ever tasted. "What is it?" I breathed.

"Ice water," she said around the ice cube in her mouth, looking not at me but over my head at her friends, a half-smile on her face.

That night my father came to see me while I was having my bath, and I asked him to get me some ice water. He brought me some, clear and cold in the glass. It didn't look right, but I tasted it. "This isn't ice water!" I yelled, outraged. He was trying to trick me, I thought. I cried and cried for the lost sweetness, tasted once and gone, I thought, forever.

In the next place we lived, a house in the suburbs, my father would stand outside my sister's bedroom door and take pictures of her standing naked in front of the round mirror over her dressing table. I knew about the pictures—some were in the family album. I told myself they were art, like paintings in the museum.

I remember her in that house when she was fifteen and I was four, standing at the top of the stairs. My mother stood at the bottom, on the uncarpeted wood floor, yelling, furious, almost raving. I don't remember what she was saying, but I crept up beside her and said, "I'll never be like her, Mommy." And I never was, though in fact I envied my sister her beauty and her social graces, and would have been like her if I could have managed it. But in the family we had different roles. She rebelled, hoping to make our mother notice her. I tried to please, hoping to make our mother notice me. But neither of us got what we wanted.

In that house I had a pair of goldfish, my first pets. My father named them Penny and Kat, after my sister Pat and her boyfriend Kenny. Later we got a dog, a female. My father named her Joey, after my sister's boyfriend Joe.

He wanted my sister to have lots of boyfriends, and she did. Later he wanted me to have lots of boyfriends, and I did. "When you walk down the aisle and see the groom at the other end, that's when you start going steady," he would say, always in the same melodramatic cadence, exaggerating his southern accent for the occasion. This aphorism was sometimes prompted by ethical questions from me—wasn't a certain amount of loyalty owed to a steady boyfriend? No, said my father: when you walk down the aisle . . . When a boy came over to see my sister, or later to see me, my father gloated in the kitchen. When another boy came while the first was there, he chortled. Sometimes three or four were there at once, and then he went almost mad with glee.

He used to make us listen to speeches he called "finger-wrapping lessons," as in "how to wrap a man around your little finger." One of these went: "Run after a man until he notices you; then turn around and run like hell, and he'll follow."

He spoke of all our boyfriends as "men," even when they were too young to shave. "Your man"—that was how he referred to even the callowest youths.

When my sister was sixteen and I was five a young resident rotated through my father's surgical service at the hospital. He invited my parents out for dinner. "I'll bring my daughter," my father told him. "I'm trying to marry her off." When he told the story in later years, as he liked to do, he always told the part about how Nate asked around the hospital, trying to find out if my sister was ugly. And he always told the part about how when he saw her, Nate was stunned by her beauty, and never guessed she was still in high school.

My father told my sister and me that Nate's name was Gus. I didn't find out his real name for a long time, but I must have known it by the time our dog Joey had puppies. I named them after some puppies in a book I had borrowed from the library: Lucky, Star, Sugarplum, and Mouse. My father changed the name of one of the females, Sugarplum, to Natina.

At my sister's high school graduation, when she was eighteen and I was seven, my father took a picture of Nate meeting her high school boyfriend Jimmy. In the picture the boy and the man are shaking hands; the boy looks smug and arrogant, and the man scowls furiously.

My father had a picture of my sister I never saw until I was grown up and she was dead, taken by my father when she was five or six. She is posed in a big easy chair, neatly dressed in a plaid skirt and white blouse, and looking down at a book in her lap. The title of the book is *Salome: My First Two Thousand Years of Love*. By the time I saw the picture I knew that Salome was the child in the Bible whose mother prompted her to dance for King Herod, and to ask for the head of John the Baptist as her reward.

My father had the power in our family, but he saw himself as weak. He lived through his daughters: We were his knights errant, sent out on romantic quests to vanquish and humiliate his enemies, our boyfriends.

My father loved to tell a story about a friend—"an asshole," according to my father—who came to visit one day when my sister, aged six or seven, was spending the weekend with them. My sister sat on the man's lap and looked up at him with her big blue eyes and smiled shyly, and it wasn't until he got up to leave that the man discovered she had cut all the buttons off his coat with a pair of fingernail scissors.

I remember an evening we spent together the summer before she went away to college, when she was eighteen and I was seven. Our parents were out, and we sat in the living room listening to radio programs—*Inner Sanctum* and *The Sealed Book* —while she sewed name tapes on her sheets. We talked and talked, and she said, "You know, you're only a little girl, but you have a lot of good things to say. I'm going to miss you when I go away." She did not hide her jealousy of me—I knew I was the favorite child, and I knew she knew it, too, even before she told me of her bitterness at living apart from our parents until she was eight. But she was tender with me most of the time; she solicited my opinions and listened to what I said and showed an interest in my life. I felt real when I was with her.

When she went away I carried her high school graduation

picture with me. Masses of blond hair, big eyes, the bittersweet smile: "She looks like a movie star!" my friends would say, looking at the picture. When she called long distance, I would cry and be unable to speak to her. Once I prepared a script ahead of time, but she departed from it and then I didn't know what to say, and I cried again.

At college she was pinned to two boys at once, a Kappa Sig and a Sigma Chi. According to Family History she was elected Sweetheart of Sigma Chi, and then the fraternity was put on probation for some prank and couldn't have the ball, and so she was saved from discovery just in time.

While she was away at college my father got a photograph of Nate, had it enlarged bigger than life-size, mounted it on black-and-white checkered cloth that showed through the face in the portrait, framed it in a grotesquely huge frame, and sent it off to her. Just so, years later, he replaced a picture of one of my boyfriends in his military school uniform with a newspaper clipping of a bulldog in a soldier suit. To represent the flowery Spanish inscription on the original, my father had written on the dog's picture: *"Siempre, Manuel."* I laughed when I saw it, and he heard me laughing and came to laugh with me—just me and my daddy, still crazy after all those years.

I learned he was not my sister's father a few days before her wedding to Nate, when I was nine. "Where's Pat?" I yelled, ranging through the house. "Where's Pat?" My mother made me sit down on the living room sofa, and she sat next to me. In a high, false voice, the same voice she used to answer questions like "What's a bidet?" she told me a story about how sometimes, a man and a woman get married, but then things don't work out and they decide not to be married anymore. That had happened to her, my mother, and so it turned out that in addition to our Daddy, my sister had Another Daddy, and that was where she had gone, to see this Other Daddy. I had never suspected his existence until that moment. I knew this was important news, because of my mother's tone of voice, but I couldn't see why, and it did not occur to me to ask: How often did she see this Other Daddy? Did he send her presents on her birthday? Did he come to see her in the hospital when she had her appendix out? I had no interest in this Other Daddy. She was my sister, and I was her sister, and that was solid; it had nothing to do with how many Daddies she had.

One night before the wedding I was considering how strange it was that women took their husbands' names. Why not the reverse? "Nate Ervin, Nate Ervin," I said aloud, pondering the sound of it. Nate heard me and took me aside. "Talking about a man that way is like calling him a dirty name," he told me. His manner was grave but kind. "You don't understand why now, but someday you will." As the years passed I thought of his words occasionally, and wondered when I would get old enough to understand.

She got married in September, on my father's birthday. All summer I had gone around gloating: "I'm getting her room. I'm getting her phone." But at the end of the wedding reception, when she and Nate got into the car and drove away, I cried and cried in a hemorrhage of grief. She was gone forever, I thought, and I was left alone with my parents.

But soon they were home again, to spend a few days with us before they moved to the valley town where Nate would do his residency. The morning they were due to arrive my father wired bells to the bedsprings in the guest room, my old bedroom. He told the story for years afterwards. I didn't understand the joke at the time, but I knew it was supposed to be funny, so I laughed whenever I heard it.

They lived in the valley for several years, and then, when she was twenty-two and I was eleven, they came back to Burlingame. Nate was ready to begin private practice as a surgeon like my father. They had little money, Nate had few patients, and so they lived with us while he was getting started, down in the old rumpus room just below the bedroom that had once been hers and now was mine.

We bickered during that time, the only time in our lives we did. At the dinner table she would pick at me, as I saw it, and I would rise, very dignified, and say, "May I be excused, please?" Sometimes I would listen at the top of the stairs while she told my mother she had to do something about my bad manners and boorish eating habits. But the mornings were cozy. We got up and ate breakfast together after my father had left for surgery, a soft-boiled egg apiece, just the two of us, while my mother slept. They stayed with us for a year, and then moved to a small apartment ten minutes away. After they left I ate breakfast alone.

Nate drank a lot, and it was a family saying that he liked to stay at a party until the last dog was hung, and cut down, and kicked, and if it rolled over, the party would go on. I used to repeat that to my friends, imagining that I was very witty and sophisticated.

The summer she was twenty-four and I was thirteen, we spent a day at a country club with some hard-drinking friends of my parents. We swam until long after dark, and then piled into several cars to continue the party at the friends' house. My friend Gail Ann and I rode in the backseat of someone's car, and Nate rode in the front. We were all still in bathing suits, and as we drove through the dark, hilly, winding streets, he reached over the seat and put his hand into the top of my bathing suit. I pulled it out and held on, trying to stop him from touching me again. He moved his hand down between my legs. With both my hands, pushing with all my might, I pushed his hand an inch or two away from my body. His fingers, thick and blunt, moved between my thighs and plucked at the crotch of my bathing suit. At last we arrived at the house, and he stopped. Later I told Gail Ann, and we rolled our eyes at each other and didn't know what to say for a minute. We didn't speak of it again, and I never told anyone else until I told my husband when I was grown.

Years after my sister died, when I was in my late twenties, my father told me Nate had affairs and so did Pat, though I don't know how my father knew. She had always been wild, my father said. She had gotten pregnant in high school, and my father had been hard put to find someone to do the abortion, he told me, in those days before it was legal. But he managed, he told me, not that she thanked him for it. She was never interested in books or ideas, the way the rest of the family was, he said; she wanted only money and possessions. He presented her to me as devious and manipulative, almost a whore. He liked to tell the story of how she said she didn't need to go to college, because she was beautiful and would easily find a man to take care of her. My father was proud of his rejoinder: "All you get out of being beautiful," he told her, "is corns on your ass."

Recently I learned that my mother, not my father, had arranged the abortion. I wonder what other lies he told me, and whether he believed she was devious and manipulative or only wanted me to believe it. Certainly he never acknowledged that he was the one who taught her to exploit men.

She and Nate became friendly with another, older couple, and soon they were spending all their free time together, eating in expensive restaurants—Nate was no longer poor, and Max was rich—drinking in nightclubs, traveling to resorts.

The summer when she was thirty and I was nineteen, she borrowed a dress from me to wear on a weekend trip she was taking in a few days. Nate was going to a medical meeting, she said, and she had decided to visit a woman friend of hers in San Diego while he was away. She was not going to tell Nate about the trip, she told me, so I was not to mention it to him either. She gave me a reason that sounded plausible, and which I promptly forgot. One night a day or two later, when I was eating dinner with them, she admired something I was wearing, and I said, "You can take this with you to San Diego too." Then I must have looked stricken and horrified, and Nate said, "San Diego?" She had planned to meet Max there, of course, though I didn't suspect it at the time. I had taken what she said at face value. She wasn't mad at me; she said it wasn't fair for her to put that burden of secrecy on me.

One day she invited me to have lunch in Sausalito. We stopped on the way in a motel parking lot, and got out of her Cadillac and into Max's, which was waiting for us. He took us to a sun-filled restaurant overlooking the yacht harbor, where the waiters treated him like the millionaire he was. He and my sister gazed into each other's eyes, and he said to me, in his thick Russian accent, "I love this woman." She had told me by then that she was unhappy with Nate, and I told myself this was all terribly glamorous and romantic.

She rented a house on the Nevada side of Lake Tahoe and moved there for the summer. The official story was that this was a vacation, and Nate was coming up on weekends. It was true that Nate was coming up on weekends, but it was also true that she was establishing residence for a Nevada divorce. One weekend I went up to visit her. After dinner, while Nate sat in the living room, my sister lay on her bed and talked to Max on the telephone. He was threatening to drive up there and confront Nate, and she was begging him not to. She sobbed as she begged him, while I ran the shower so Nate wouldn't hear. Although I didn't know much, I knew enough to know that Max was enjoying her tears.

Max did come to visit, after Nate had left, and when it was time for me to leave he drove me over the mountains to the

Reno airport. He took the curves at full speed in his huge Cadillac. I clutched the padded door handle and prayed. He looked over at me and smiled.

At the end of the summer my sister drove to Reno for the day and divorced her husband. I was home when she called from Tahoe, crying, and asked to speak to my father. He wouldn't come to the phone. He sat in his big easy chair in the living room and wouldn't answer when I begged him to speak to her.

The summer after that, she married Max. I was her maid of honor and her closest friend, but she only hinted, as the months passed, about his jealousy and her unhappiness. A week before she died, she called me and told me she wanted to leave the marriage, but she was afraid Max wouldn't let her go. She had no money of her own, and she had been totally dependent on men, "her men," all her life. Perhaps she thought her only hope was to find a man to rescue her who was richer, more powerful, nastier, and more aggressive than Max, as Max had rescued her from Nate, as Nate, perhaps, had rescued her from my father.

Then one evening just at twilight, Max pulled out to pass another driver on a narrow country road, drove his Cadillac head-on into an oncoming car, and killed them both. She was thirty-three and I was twenty-two. I slept and woke in tears, over and over through the night and the following nights. For months and years afterwards something would remind me of her and I'd start to cry for my loss. For although we had never talked about our parents' drinking, about our father's seductive behavior in public, about the things he did to us in secret, still she was my ally. She was the only one in the world who knew what life with my parents was like.

The church was crowded for the memorial service, and afterwards we stood in the back for what seemed like hours as people filed by and hugged us and kissed us. And then we went back to my parents' apartment, and my father announced that we should all stop grieving now. "It's time to close the book," he said, frowning and using the controlled, angry voice that said we must not argue with him.

SEX

It was 1960. I was eighteen, home for the summer after my freshman year in college. My boyfriend was pressuring me to go to bed with him, and one night I sat down with my parents and said, "You've never told me what you think about premarital sex. What *do* you think?" Although I didn't say so, I was asking them to give me a reason for refusing to sleep with him. They gave me abstractions in which I could find no help or even meaning: sentences that began "When two people love each other and the time is right . . ."

I started to cry. "But what do you say when somebody wants you to go to bed with him?" I sobbed.

49

"You just say 'I don't want to,' " my mother said, her voice full of spurious confidence.

But that was just what I could not say, not without confirming my boyfriend's charge that I was a frigid prude, not a real woman. I knew there was something wrong with me because I didn't like sex.

The awful question, the one I could not bring myself to ask my parents, was "What if you *do* want to?" The idea of admitting to anyone that I might someday want someone to touch me "there" was too awful. It was not, in any case, relevant to my inner debate. I didn't want to sleep with my boyfriend. But if I couldn't come up with a good reason for refusing, I guessed I was going to have to do it.

Later each of my parents came to me privately for a serious talk. My mother told me I should think very carefully before I did anything. My father said that there was nothing wrong with premarital sex, but that I should be sure to do it someplace private and comfortable: in a bed, not in a car. And I should be sure to use birth control. "Your man," he told me, should wear a condom, and I should use contraceptive jelly—he wrote down the brand name, Ortho-Gynol—and after the first time I should go to a doctor—he wrote down a name—and be fitted with a diaphragm.

I reported all this to my boyfriend, and a week later we made our way to a motel, after stopping at a drugstore to buy condoms and Ortho-Gynol. I did not enjoy the experience, wished I hadn't done it, hoped I wouldn't have to do it again, feared that having done it once, it would be even harder to escape a second time. The next night, overcome with guilt, I crept into my father's bed, snuggled up to his naked body as I had done on so many Sunday mornings as a child, and told him what I had done.

My mother was spending a few days with a friend, so my

father and I were alone. He tried to comfort me by repeating that there was nothing wrong with premarital sex, and by telling me that he and my mother had lived together for six months before they were married. Somehow this was not comforting: The idea of living with, and then marrying, my boyfriend was depressing, to say the least.

And there was something about his tone of voice. . . . I remembered a conversation at dinner not long before when a friend—a boy, but not a boyfriend—asked my father for his views on premarital sex. My father said there was nothing wrong with it, "when two people love each other and the time is right . . ." He paused. "But I have to admit, when I think of *my Betsy* . . ." He shuddered.

Now, in his bed, as he told me I hadn't done anything wrong, his words seemed meant to reassure me, but his voice let me know I had betrayed him.

I left his bed and went to my room. But I couldn't settle down, and I went back to his room. "I have a stomachache," I said. "I feel all full and bloated. Is there anything I can do for that?" He was a doctor, after all.

He suggested an enema, and got the apparatus out of the closet for me. I went into my bathroom and fiddled around with it, but I didn't know what to do. I went back to his room. I had taken off my clothes so I wouldn't get them wet, and I didn't get dressed again. Unlike my mother and sister, I was not casual about nudity, not usually. But in that moment I felt somehow that putting on my clothes would mean that I had something to be ashamed of; or afraid of.

"I can't figure out how to do it," I said.

"I'll help you," he said.

He gave me the enema as I kneeled naked on the bathroom floor.

"YOU ARE
NOT AT ALL
AS HE THINKS
YOU ARE"

Three months after I slept with my boyfriend, my father had a heart attack. He wrote this letter while he was recovering. On the outside of the envelope he wrote: "Dearest Betsy, Today I felt like writing you a letter to be read when you are about to be married, so I wrote it realizing that it may be premature. You may read it now or you can save it until the time you need it. Love, Pa."

I read it right away. I did not wait until I "needed" it. I did not understand why it left me feeling so desolate.

My Darling Betsy—

This man of yours has in his mind & subconscious a picture that is completely unreal & unobtainable. Part of his love for you is due to just meeting at the right time & part is due to your awareness of this picture, either by that special sense some women have, or possibly you just listened when he described it. At any rate you have convinced him that it is of you, & shortly you will be married, for better or for worse as the ceremony goes. You now have less than a year to show him that home is a pleasant place, a happy place, an interesting place, at times a refuge, & that your bed & board is the best there is. These are a few of the ingredients of married love which must soon replace the romantic love you now know & properly treasure. There are other ingredients which you will learn possibly better than I. But start to teach him these things now & he may never notice that you are not at all as he thinks you are, or if he does it will be with pleasure & not bitterness.

Nor is he as you have pictured him. But the job is principally yours — at this stage he will not even suspect these things—later, perhaps yes. This is part of the Comedy of Life: the man must always play the lead but the woman sets the stage & in each scene she must guide him into the proper position to function in this dominant role assigned to him or he will fail— this slip is deliberately Freudian & you will learn that an episode in your physical love recapitulates the entire play.

And good luck to you both.

Love
Papa

NIGHT
TERRORS

When I was a child, six, seven, eight years old, I used to lie awake watching the spots on the ceiling to see if they moved. If they didn't move, maybe they weren't spiders. If they did move, they were spiders, and if I slept, they would crawl down the wall and into the bed. I imagined that while I slept a spider would crawl between my legs and up into my vagina, and I wouldn't know it was there, or if I did know I would be powerless to stop it: No matter how hard I squeezed my legs together it would crawl into me.

Sometimes as a teenager I woke up unable to breathe;

sometimes I still do. I sit up in bed, gasping for breath, my throat almost closed, my heart pounding.

Sometimes after I was married I dreamed knives were coming down from the ceiling, or spiders were lowering themselves to the bed on threads of silk; or a crack was opening up in the ceiling and chunks of plaster were about to fall on the bed; or a corpse hung from a rope and twisted slowly over my head. Something was coming from above to get me. I had these dreams and didn't know why. I still have them, but now I do know why.

When I began to be afraid that my father had done something to me—I wasn't sure what—my dreams got worse. I dreamed that my husband had a secret life, which he entered through the door of his bedside table. While I slept he withdrew from me, leaving me alone and vulnerable, at the mercy of the man coming heavily up the stairs, closer, closer, until he was standing over the bed, reaching out his hand to touch me as I desperately pretended to be asleep.

Even now sometimes I dream the man in the bed with me is not my husband, but a stranger. The stranger is asleep, but soon he will wake. He has gotten rid of my husband and taken his place in the bed, and I am at his mercy. While I slept I have been pressing my body against his, thinking he is my husband, but he is not. I've been acting shameless, pressing my body against the body of a naked stranger. He'll think I desire him; by pressing against him I gave him the right to do whatever he wanted to me. It's too late to go back; I've committed myself. I didn't know he was a stranger, but I should have known. It's my fault: I let him get into the bed, I pressed myself against him, I had no right to resist whatever he wanted to do to me. I can't get away.

When I began to remember what my father had done to me, I began to dream that I'd forgotten to feed my dogs. I still have this dream. Almost every night, even now, I wake with a start; sometimes I jump out of bed, shouting aloud, "Oh, God!" Sometimes I think the dogs are in the closet; they've been shut away without food or water for days, dying of hunger and thirst. I have to take care of them, right now!

I am the caretaker. I have an urgent and pressing reason to get out of bed, out from under the knives, away from the naked stranger. It's a legitimate excuse: I'm sorry, I can't let you touch me between my legs because I have to feed my dogs. It's a matter of life and death, their life and death. If I don't feed them, they'll die. You understand, don't you? You aren't going to let those innocent dogs suffer, are you? It wouldn't be right, it wouldn't be kind. So let me go and feed them. And maybe by the time I get back you'll be gone. Or maybe somebody will hear me in the kitchen and come to help me and I won't be alone anymore, defending myself with my duty to the dogs.

I am the dogs: alone in the dark, hungry and thirsty and totally dependent on the good will of the people who are supposed to take care of me, who have forgotten to take care of me, who have left me alone and hungry and thirsty in the dark.

Why are the dogs in the closet? We got them to protect us against intruders—why aren't they ripping the bastard's throat out? Because they know him. Because they depend on him, because he's the one who buys their food, the one who decides whether they go or stay. He's got all the power. So they won't rip his throat out or even sound an alarm; they'll just let him creep silently toward me in the night while they cower there in the closet and never make a noise.

I am in the closet, hiding in the dark. He can't find me here. But my mother can't find me either. She won't find me, because she's not looking for me, and I can't call out to her. I have to stay very, very quiet, or he'll hear me, he'll come after me, he'll open the door and come in and find me, and I won't be able to get away. There isn't anywhere else to hide. I want my mommy. I want her to look and look until she finds me. If she finds me first it'll be okay. He won't be able to get me; she'll protect me. But she isn't looking for me. She has to rest. I keep pestering her, wanting her to pay attention to me, and she can't take it; she has to rest. If I push too hard she'll just stop taking care of me. She'll put me in the closet and let me die.

I am the caretaker, and my mother is in the closet, hungry and thirsty and alone. She needs me. She needs me to take care of her. She is far too fragile to protect me; it's my job to protect her.

I am the predator, the man who is coming in the night. I am walking heavily up the stairs. I am looking in the door. I am standing over the bed. The child is soft and tender between her legs. I touch her there. It's our secret—nobody knows; nobody will ever know. What if she tells? She won't tell. But if she does? I'll say she was dreaming. It's best when she doesn't wake up. She just has a wonderful dream about a wonderful lover who gives her wonderful feelings between her legs, and she thinks it's just a dream and she never wakes up and she never remembers. But I can watch her twitch and jerk on the strings I pull. She's my doll baby, my little doll. I can play with her whenever I want.

Night after night I fight sleep, startling wide-awake whenever my head nods. At last I sleep. Twenty minutes later I gasp and sit up, or jump out of bed: the knives, or the suffocation, or the stranger, or the dogs in the closet. Sometimes the cycle repeats itself two or three times during the night. And sometimes there are other dreams.

I am in a resort cottage, on vacation with my whole family: my husband, my parents, my grandfather and his wife, my sister and her husband, my aunt and uncle. The cottage is one big bare room, with a shiny brown floor. There are many bathrooms opening off the main room. But none of the toilets work. Some have been taken out and replaced with wastebaskets. All the toilets and all the wastebaskets are full to the brim with shit. And everyone is acting very cheerful and happy, their voices high and false, pretending that everything in the cottage is just as it should be.

I am in a big house with wide stairways and a glass-paneled door. In the kitchen a man is putting up big sheets of black plastic. He is outfitting a darkroom. There are kerosene lanterns mounted on the wall. There are several women in the house. One of them lies naked on an iron cot. I am under the cot, hiding. The man talks dirty to us. The woman loves it. I feel aroused, but terrified. I wrap my legs around my purse and my zippered canvas bag to keep them from being taken away from me, as my clothes were. I need them to escape. The naked woman chases me with a needle. She pricks me in the neck. I grab the needle and push it into the roof of her mouth. "Oh, God!" she moans, ecstatic. I run away, through an old man's house, small and jammed with furniture, in the front door and out the glass-paneled door in back. In my bathrobe I try to fly in the night through bare trees that grab at me, over the back streets.

I deliver two babies, without pain. Then my belly splits open. There is a hole into my abdominal cavity; I can look in and see a third baby trying to come out. I look again, and now the baby looks like a wedge of cabbage. I push it back in. I go to see my surgeon with my mother. He examines me in a kitchen on a wooden table. It's a cursory exam, but he is nice to me. He says he is surprised to see how much subcutaneous fat I have. I see that now the abdominal cavity is not open; there's just a slit in the fat, an inch or two deep, all fat along the edges. My mother tries to speak and can't; just gibberish comes out. She coughs and tries again, but it's no good. The surgeon comes closer and murmurs, "Something is wrong with your mother." He doesn't examine her or make any suggestions about what to do. He washes his hands, still encased in yellow Playtex gloves, at the kitchen sink.

I'm with my father, swimming in a drainage canal with steep cement sides. The water is clear and blue, but I keep saying, "It's dirty. It'll make us sick. My incision will get infected." He keeps saying, "Don't worry." Then I'm at school, in a classroom with a big fat teacher who says, "Do you want to take the class?" I stand up, read a poem aloud, and ask one of the students a question about it. She says, "I don't have it in my book." I look in my book and the poem is gone. The class is silent and hostile. I let them go early. I go home and they have been in my house and moved all the furniture, even the bathroom fixtures. I go to the bathroom, then realize I can't flush the toilet because it isn't hooked up. I come out of the bathroom, and the students appear from hiding places and make themselves at home. They make a mess, and they won't leave.

I am a small child in bed with an older girl, thirteen or so. There is another girl or woman in the bed with us. We don't want her to know about our sex play. There are stuffed animals in the bed, and a security blanket. We are my father's three daughters.

I am with a companion: my mother, or my sister. She is protecting me from the surgeon, who is down at the end of a dead-end road, waiting to kill with his bloody knife anyone who goes down there. We stand at the head of the road, next to a roadblock, and tell people that it's safe to pass. We both know this is a lie: Anyone who goes down the road will be mutilated and killed. But if we don't protect him, he'll do it to us. If I don't help my mother protect him, she'll choose him instead of me, no matter what the danger to me. She will refuse to protect me. Now my companion is my sister, my peer and ally. She doesn't know what to do, and I don't know what to do, but we are trying to save ourselves. I know this is a dream, and I give myself a chance to end the dream my way. I propose to my sister that we kill him. We do kill him. We kill him over and over, but when we go back to look he is alive again, waiting for us. I propose that we drive a stake through his heart so he'll stay dead. But I don't believe it will work. He is powerful and I am helpless and so are my allies. No one believes what the surgeon has done. He waits at the end of the road to mutilate me.

The dreams continue, even now. Every night I lie awake, fighting sleep. I breathe deeply, and relax, and then my breath catches on the exhale and I'm wide awake again, gasping. My therapist has told me I'm safe now. "I'm safe," I say to myself, over and over like a mantra. But I don't feel safe. It is like believing the earth is flat and knowing it's round at the same time. I know my father isn't coming to my bed this night. I know he is dead. And I know the man next to me in the bed is my husband, who loves me. But I am back in the low, soft bed of my childhood, waiting for my father. He will drop from the ceiling or appear in the bed next to me, an incubus. I am certain that if I sleep, my father will come and violate me, like the spider in my childhood fantasies. He has ceased to exist, but he will come after me and he will get me and there will be nothing I can do to stop him. My borders are not secure: He is within.

REMEMBERING:
ONE

Remembering may have begun on the day in therapy when I began to talk about sex. Or maybe it began on the morning, a few days later, when I woke up full of new shame about an old incident, the time my father gave me an enema when I was eighteen. Or maybe it began after that, with the dreams which grew more frightening as Kris and I focused more on my father.

But in my mind remembering began with a box of letters my mother found in the basement of her house when she was getting ready to sell it: almost a year after I started therapy; eight years after my father died; more than forty years after the first time he molested me.

Inside the lid was pasted a note in his handwriting: "This manuscript is prepared expressly for my daughter Betsy Ervin. If I should die before giving it to her it should be given to her promptly without being opened. It contains no instructions, will, or other material of interest or value to anyone else, and some of the material is personal for the two of us."

I could hear the irritation in my mother's voice as she told me about the box, and I sympathized with her. I remembered the time, after I was married, when my father sent me a draft of his novel so I could read and comment on it. When they came to visit and I sat down with my father to talk about the manuscript, he told me that he had not showed it to my mother. "I don't know why I didn't," he said. "I showed it to"—he named a woman he'd been carrying on a flirtation with for a number of years—"but for some reason I just didn't want to show it to your mother." The protagonist of his novel, ironically named Manly Peters, had much in common with this woman's husband.

I asked him once if he was sleeping with this woman and he said he wasn't, but I didn't believe him. So when I heard about the box of letters I thought it was probably evidence of their affair. I wasn't surprised that he wanted to save this evidence for me—it seemed very much in character. But I was angry. My father had involved himself too much in my life while he lived. I did not want to be touched by his dead hand.

It took my mother three weeks to get to the post office with the box. While I waited I became conscious of a growing anxiety. What if there was something worse than what I expected in the box? But what could be worse?

I developed an ear infection that plugged up both ears so I could hardly hear. Maybe it was just a coincidence, my first ear infection in forty years. Or maybe my body was sending a message: *Don't tell me. I don't want to hear.*

Something about my sister. Something about my father and my sister. Something that lay behind the sexy pictures he took of her, and the way she walked around the house with no clothes on, even as an adult. Of course he would never have done anything to me, I told myself, but she was his stepdaughter. She matured early. She was seductive. She adored him, I told myself—at least that's what my mother always said. As the days passed I became more and more afraid that when I opened the box I would discover that my father had slept with my sister.

One day I was jogging near our house, pondering this terrible possibility, sounding the depth of my fear. Suddenly, as I crossed a wide, oak-shaded boulevard, a thought came into my mind as if it had been projected on a screen: *I'm afraid my father did something to me.*

I began to cry, and the tears mingled with my sweat as I stumbled along. Yes, this was it. This was what I was afraid of.

I lived with the fear for two or three days. I don't remember what I did. I must have fixed meals, fed the dogs, taken showers, washed clothes. I must have spent a good deal of time with Tom, who was nine; William was away at camp. I didn't want to think about my fears, but I did think about them; I thought of little else. I did not talk to anyone about what I was feeling. In a few days I would tell my husband; but for now I held my fear close to me, as if it were a small, helpless animal I was protecting from the cold.

On Sunday my husband took Tom canoeing. Alone in the house, I set about confronting my fear. If there was incest, when did it happen? What caused it to happen? Could I find any traces of it in my memory or the documents I had from the past?

I worked in my bedroom, a warm, bright room up at the top of the house. Through the window over my desk I could see the green leaves of the plum tree in our front yard. I moved back and forth between my desk and my closet, pulling musty boxes from the shelves and spreading their contents on the soft brown carpet. I had my baby book, *Our Baby's First Seven Years*, filled with snapshots taken by my father and detailed entries in his almost illegible doctor's scribble ("[she] distinguished between boys and girls easily at 2 yrs"). And I had my father's autobiography, a 193-page unpublished *Letter to Betsy* he wrote for me after I was married. I started listing important dates in our family history on sheets of paper torn from my notebook: When did we move from the army base to the apartment? When did my father go overseas? When did I go to nursery school? As I read the words my father had written for me, I decided that the most likely date for the incest—I hypothesized a single incident—was November 1945, when my father returned from the Pacific. I was three. His autobiography told of his anxiety about the future during that time, his fear that he would be unable to find a job, his perception that he had been emasculated by the army: "With its regimentation and enforced dependence on authority," he wrote, the army "saps a man's confidence in himself. It takes a long time to learn again to stand straight and walk like a man."

So perhaps it had happened—if it had happened—in the apartment in San Francisco, when my father came back from the war. But when I searched my memory I found I could hardly place my father in that apartment. I had only two memories of him there, one of the day of his return, another of the evening he brought the glass of ice water to me in the bathtub. I thought we had moved from there as soon as he came back, but I found when I looked at the records that we lived there for seven more months after he came home. Why was it so hard to remember him there, when I had some earlier memories of him and many later ones?

I pored over the baby book and *Letter to Betsy* for hours, scribbling notes, trying to put together a scenario of what might have happened. A worst-case scenario, I called it in my thoughts, though I carefully avoided filling in any scenes in my mind. "Incest" was what I called it, an abstraction without content. As I worked I felt feverish. My head seemed larger than normal, and filled with air. The only feeling I was conscious of was a sense of urgency: I wanted to *know*. If it turned out that "it" had happened, I wanted to be prepared.

"I have this story to tell you," I said to Kris, my therapist, several days later. We had been working together for almost a year now, first on my relationship with my children, and more recently on issues about my parents. I hesitated, and then I said, "I don't know if I made it up or if it's real."

She listened. "It feels like a story to you," she said, "because when something like that happens, everybody acts like it didn't."

"You mean it might really have happened?" Now I wasn't sure I really did want to know.

There was a good chance it had happened, she said. It was consistent with what I remembered about my father and my relationship with him, and with the dreams I had been having, and with the difficulties I had being close to my children, and also, she said, with the feelings I had during and after sex with my husband: If I enjoyed our lovemaking, invariably I would pick a fight with him afterwards. More often I would tune out during sex, and plot how to rearrange my closet or improve my accounting system. Other times I imagined vivid scenes in which I had surgery for cancer in my breasts or genitals, but failed to recover and died a lingering, painful death, rotting away from within. Or else I imagined my husband dying of a heart attack: suddenly, as we made love, crying out and then going limp, a heavy, lifeless weight crushing my chest. I would

65

have caused his death. And then I would be left alone with our children, unable to care for them or myself.

But how could I forget something so important?

People do, she said. It's very common for sexual abuse victims to repress their memories of the experience; it's one of the things they do to survive. If it had happened, she said, memories would come.

When the box of letters finally arrived, it was an anticlimax. It contained, along with some innocuous letters and poems, the expected evidence of my father's affair: five love poems written by a woman to my father, including one called "Five Days, Four Nights," which described a tryst in a mountain cabin and contained references to tangled sheets and tangled legs. When, a year later, I told my mother about them, she said they were not written by the woman I thought had written them, but another woman my father had been carrying on with during the same period. My mother knew where the mountain cabin was and when they had gone there.

I shut down. For six months I had no dreams about incest, and read no books about it. I became very cheerful; I felt competent. I decided to terminate therapy.

Then the dreams started again, more specific and terrifying than ever. I went back to therapy and began to write about what I thought had happened to me, to fill in the blanks in that worst-case scenario. I was afraid, but I wanted to know, and I hoped the writing would help.

I had no memory of what my father had done to me, so I tried to reconstruct it. I put all my skill—as reporter, novelist, scholar—to work making that reconstruction as accurate and vivid as possible. I used the memories I had to get to the memories I didn't have: I had not forgotten the way my father looked during that time in our lives, his smooth round face, his steel-rimmed glasses. I used also my knowledge of my father's character—the way he loved the role of teacher and his calm, didactic way of presenting information. And I used what I knew of myself, my own shame about my sexuality. As I struggled against that shame to get a clear visual image of my genitals as the object of my father's abuse, I realized that I had always believed, without knowing how it might have happened, that my body had been breached and damaged long ago, and could never be whole again. I tried to account for all that I knew and all that I remembered. The story I wrote I called "Surgeon's Hands."

SURGEON'S
HANDS

H e had beautiful hands. Very
large, with very long, graceful fingers and long, double-jointed
thumbs. A surgeon's hands. You just had to look at them to see
that. He was very good with his hands. He could make anything: He made my first Halloween costume when I was four, a
ghost with shoulders on a wire frame that towered above my
head, and a jack-o'-lantern on top that I could light up with a
switch in my hand.

He came home from the war in November 1945, when I
was three and a half. He was one of many returning servicemen,

all looking for work. He wanted to teach, but there was no place for him. He had always taken what was offered, gone down whatever road opened up before him. Now he was afraid there would be no offers; he seemed to be facing a dead end. We went on with our lives, but we were all afraid.

An afternoon in November, soon after his return. My mother and my sister are out. I am taking my nap, upstairs in my room, the room I share with my sister. A bare room: bare wood floor, my sister's bed, my crib, plain sheer white curtains at the windows. A plain ceiling fixture, a square of frosted glass concealing two light bulbs. A chest of drawers. A mirror. My toy chest.

I sleep, in shirt and underpants; my corduroy overalls hang over the end of my crib. My thumb is in my mouth. Little wisps of hair have escaped from my braids. My head rests on a folded quilted cotton mattress pad—my mother has told me that sleeping with my head on a pillow would ruin my posture. The pad smells clean, familiar.

I sleep soundly. My father stands beside the crib and looks down at me.

I turn over in my sleep, onto my back. He puts his hand on my chest; perhaps he's thinking about how small I am, how fragile—what if I just stopped breathing? He pushes harder, his big hand almost covering my chest, his middle finger pushing hard against what will someday be my left breast. I wake.

I see his smooth-shaven round face, his dark, deep-set eyes, his nose that makes a T with his straight eyebrows, his straight mouth. He breathes heavily, the way he would sometimes in later years when he pulled my pants down and spanked me, so angry I'd be afraid he was going to kill me.

Behind his glasses, the almost invisible steel-rimmed army

glasses, his eyes are unfocused. I wonder if he's been asleep, awakened from a nap as I'd awakened him once, a year or so earlier, before he went away and came back. That other time he'd come into my room, scowling, wearing a gray sweatshirt and no pants, his penis hanging down like an elephant's trunk, and ordered me to go back to sleep and stop bothering him. Did I call out in my sleep, this November afternoon? Now he is fully dressed, and he isn't scowling. He has a funny smile on his face. His mouth hangs a little open—he looks stupid, not smart like I know he is. I can see the wet insides of his lips, and his tongue, wide and flat, resting between them.

He stands above me, looking down. I'm at the bottom of a box, a deep box, like the sandbox outside the laundry room in our apartment complex. But I'm not abandoned, as I thought I was in the sandbox. I'm in my crib and Daddy is here.

The hand that woke me is still on my chest, pressing too hard. He takes it away, but I can still feel the pressure of his middle finger. He moves his hand down to the crotch of my cotton underpants. His long fingers move between the elastic and my thigh. I picture the place in my mind's eye: a line between two fat humps, like two big soft fingers pressed together. The pee comes out a hole in between.

Those long fingers lift up my underpants, move underneath them, spread apart those things between my legs like fingers, like fat lips. He takes his hand away, licks his middle finger, puts it back into my pants. He starts to speak in a gentle monotone, his southern accent slurring the consonants and extending the vowels. "You have a little bump here—it's called your clitoris, and you can touch it and make yourself feel good." He moves his finger, wet from his spit, up and down. It feels wonderful, better than anything I ever imagined, but I squeeze my legs together. "Don't worry," he says. "I won't hurt you. I wouldn't hurt you for anything in the world." His voice is soft, soothing, his doctor voice.

"It feels good, doesn't it? You like it, don't you?" I do like it, I want him to keep doing it, but I want him to stop too. It's too much; it feels too much.

He lifts up my bottom and pulls my underpants off. I lie there exposed, my shirt not long enough to cover me. He licks his fingers and lets them crawl over me, over those parts of my body I didn't know the names of before. "These are your labia —that's the Latin for lips. Labia majora, big lips; labia minora, little lips. And this little bump is your clitoris."

He presses his body against the bars of my crib. I feel something like a Fourth of July sparkler in the place he called my clitoris, flaring and flaring again. It feels too strong; I twist away from it. My flesh feels tender, fragile. He licks his finger and tickles me with it, there. "Just lie still. Just relax—you're not doing anything wrong."

If I'm not doing anything wrong, why is he telling me I'm not doing anything wrong? I lie there with his fingers crawling over me. I keep jerking, I can't help it, jerking under his fingers. I think it hurts, but I'm not sure. My flesh is so soft down there, so different from the firm skin all over the rest of me, he must be hurting me.

His finger moves faster, presses harder. It feels big, as big as his penis looked that other time he came to my room, scowling, angry with me. He rubs against the bars of the crib and his eyes cross and roll up behind his glasses. Suddenly he groans and slumps over the bars. His finger stops moving. Is he dead?

No: He lifts his head and looks at me.

"Did you like it? Did it feel good?" I know he wants me to say yes. I nod my head. He clears his throat with a single barking cough. "It would be better not to say anything about this to your mother. There's nothing wrong with what you did, but she

71

might not understand." I don't wonder why we can't just explain whatever she doesn't understand. I already know that "wouldn't understand" doesn't mean anything except "would be mad." She'd be mad at me.

When Daddy was gone I thought everything would be perfect when he came home. My mother would stop being silent and withdrawn; she would be happy—we would all be happy. But it hasn't happened. And now something's wrong; I don't know what. She still frowns and looks mad; she still doesn't listen when I talk to her. I know not to pester her; she gets mad when I do that. Maybe it's my fault that whatever it was didn't happen when he came home.

He leaves me in my crib. I hear him in the bathroom, then walking heavily into the room next to mine. I have to go to the bathroom. Is it okay to get up and do it? I don't want to see him, lying on the bed in their room. But I have to go, bad. Finally, I climb out of my crib. But I waited too long. Before I can get to the bathroom I feel warm pee running down my bare leg. I wet myself. I feel so ashamed. And it hurts—it burns that place my daddy touched. I sit on the toilet and finish going, and wipe myself. That place keeps on hurting. I put my hand down there. Those things he named . . . they feel like soft noodles, all jumbled together. I can't picture in my mind what they look like. And I can't see them, even when I bend my head over until it touches the toilet seat. I touch the little bump where the sparkler feeling was, where it hurts now. It feels like a soft cork in a hole. I knew about the hole the pee comes out of, but I didn't know about this hole. It must reach right up into the inside of me.

I go back in my room and climb back into my crib. It still hurts down there. I must have done something to myself, opened something up that wasn't supposed to be open. That crack between those two fat lips used to be a shallow crack, but now it's deep, deep—I don't even know how far it goes.

My mother comes home. I always tell her when something hurts, but this time I don't tell her. Daddy said she wouldn't understand. Daddy said I didn't do anything wrong, but if I didn't do anything wrong, why does it hurt? I won't tell. I won't ever tell. But if I don't tell, who'll make it get better? It will get worse and worse and I'll die. The hole will get deeper and deeper, wider and wider, until there's nothing left of me.

My throat hurts, the way it hurts when I try not to cry. It hurts when I swallow. I can't eat. I won't put anything from the outside inside. I feel hot. I'm in my crib, at the bottom of a box, and my mother and father are standing over me. I'm afraid to go to sleep: I might wake up and see that smooth round face. But I do sleep, and I do wake up and see that face. He's scared. I can feel how scared he is. He's scared I'm going to die.

I'm so worried about my throat, it hurts so bad, and my chest feels thick and full, and it hurts so bad when I cough. I forget about my clitoris, the cork in the hole leading deep inside me; I forget about those lips my daddy told me about. I forget those broken parts of me are even there at all.

My daddy is a surgeon. He cuts people open. After I get well, I have to go to the hospital and get cut open. He explains it all to me, in that same gentle southern monotone, drawing me a picture of the tonsils that will be scooped out with "a little knife that looks more like a spoon." My daddy won't do it, he tells me, because daddies don't cut their own children open. I won't know what's happening, because I will be asleep.

After the operation, "You won't get sick so much," my mother tells me, her voice letting me know that my getting sick is a burden to her. My getting sick was something else she didn't understand.

73

REMEMBERING:
TWO

I read the story I had written about a November afternoon in 1945 in the Park Merced development of San Francisco, when I was three, and I began to scream and curse and cry. I cried so hard I wet my pants, and then I remembered how the urine felt that other time, running down my leg, and how it burned my genitals. I experienced again my terror and my shame, when I read the story I called "Surgeon's Hands."

But did it really happen? Did my father molest me on that November afternoon? When I wrote "Surgeon's Hands," the feelings that came up for me were so intense I felt they must be grounded in some reality. But my memories of the incident are nowhere near as organized and specific as the story. They are vague and fragmentary, and strange: In my mind's eye I see my father leaning over my crib—but what I see is the back of his head, and my own face framed by tousled braids. I feel the terror and the shame, but not the sexual contact itself. Those more specific memories are of later incidents.

At the time I wrote the story it seemed logical that if my father had ever molested me, he could only have done it at a time when his self-esteem was very low and he was under great pressure, which was the case in November 1945. I chose to believe that, if it had happened at all—and I was still reserving judgment on that—it had happened only once. One day in therapy I said—I thought I said—"The incest took place when I was three."

Kris looked at me and I could see the compassion in her face. "Are you aware," she said slowly, "that you said, 'The incest started when I was three'?"

"Oh, no," I said, and I heard my voice as if it belonged to someone else, high and thin and desperate-sounding.

It seemed impossible. Maybe, just maybe, he might have done it once—but over and over? My father, who gave people's lives back to them? It was easier, more comfortable, to believe that I was making it up, easier to say to myself that I was crazy.

"You must be crazy to think I'd do a thing like that," I heard my father say to my mother when I was eight or nine. "You need to have your head examined." She thought he was having an affair. As I struggled to remember the abuse, craving memories as proof that it had really happened, I could hear his voice saying those words to me: "You must be crazy to think I'd do a thing like that."

Over and over, I made a case for the incest having happened, and then a case against it. I wanted to believe it: I wanted not to be crazy. But I wanted not to believe it, not to believe that my father would do that to me.

Wanted or not, memories came. In the daytime, when for me it is easier to sleep, memories come. Lying on the sofa with the sun warming me like a blanket, I sink into sleep with the sense that I am literally coming down from the ceiling into a musty, dust-filled room, crowded with furniture and artifacts lying across each other in untidy piles covered with cobwebs. I sink into the welter of images, and there is a moment when one of them sharpens, and I can see it clearly. Then it drifts out of focus again and disappears.

I am in my low, narrow bed, lying on my side next to my father, and my hand is moving up and down, up and down on his penis as his hand guides mine. The image has edges, which I can't see beyond. I can't see the bed, the wall behind it, the door my father came through. I can't see my father's face. There is no affect, no muscle tension, no physical sensation, just a visual image. There is only his penis, my hand, his hand, and the motion.

I see his soft, hairy stomach, inches from my eyes. He is standing upright in front of me. I don't know how tall I am, how old I am, whether I am kneeling or standing, only that my mouth is level with his penis. But there is no penis in the image, and no mouth: The picture is cut off just below my nose.

I see a man's naked body covering a woman's body; the woman is also naked. He lies on top of her, his legs straight. She is much smaller than he is, and she looks unnaturally flat, as if his weight is pressing her shape out of her.

I see an image—perhaps it is a drawing—of a crater with soft dirt piled up around its edges. There is a cylindrical stick, like a short dowel or a section of a stick from the game of Pick Up Sticks, emerging from the crater at an angle. The stick is very hard, and the dirt is very soft.

"What does that mean to you?" my therapist asked.

"I'm afraid"—my voice kept sticking in my throat—"I'm afraid it means that somebody . . . stuck . . . something . . . into me."

"Who might have done that to you?"

"Not my father! It couldn't have been my father!"

"Why not?"

"He was a doctor! My father wouldn't do that to me!"

I am sitting on a man's lap. I am wearing a dress and his hand is under it. He is touching my clitoris with huge, blunt fingers. His fingers are so big, and my body is so small. We are sitting in a chair, and I am looking down at the floor. I can see my lap but not the shape of his hand moving under my skirt. But I can feel the intense pleasure of his touch, and the terror that goes with it.

More memories came. One day I was listening to an audiotape I had bought to improve my reading speed, but when I heard the man's voice on the tape saying, "Faster . . . faster," in a calm, didactic monotone, I started to cry and couldn't go on.

Another day, in a movement class, I heard the teacher say, "Look in the mirror." My body filled with shame and I felt as transparent as glass. I turned my head toward the mirror but I could not look.

Sometimes I get only information. Writing in my journal, I saw words pouring out of me onto the page. Without stopping to think, I wrote:

He came to our room [the room I shared with my sister in San Francisco] and said to her, "You're a woman now and it's time for you to start acting like one. I'm going to teach you to make love like a woman." She cried and begged him not to. He got into the bed with her. She struggled. He got on top of her and held her down and penetrated her, and she struggled. He put his hand over her mouth so she wouldn't be heard. But I heard, and saw, dimly, from my bed. He finished and sat up. He said to her, "The first time is always hard. But you'll learn to like it, you'll see—just like you liked the things we did when you were a little girl." After that he kept coming to our room at night, first to my bed and then to hers.

I began to realize what a profoundly, chronically angry man my father was, though I had been taught to see him as gentle and courtly, the way people outside the family did. Then I understood the dynamics of my parents' quarrels: My mother would pick at him for reasons I could never understand when I overheard them, he would maintain the patience for which he was famous, she would fuel and then dampen her rage with more and more wine. Finally, he would help her stagger to their bed, and then he would make his way to mine. After any quarrel I might find his fingers between my legs, and even when he touched me softly and skillfully, I knew he was running on rage.

One day, pondering the desperate panic I feel when my sons quarrel, I understood, in a disconnected, intellectual sort of way, that I identified their anger with my parents' rage at each other. But then I suddenly felt, as if in the present, the full force of my father's rage, turned on me: The big one is holding the little one and the little one can't get away and I am the little one and he is holding me so I can't move and he is so strong and I can't breathe, I can't breathe!

Memories are fragmentary and disconnected: a picture without a story, a story without a picture, feelings without pictures or stories. Often they are preceded by an aura: I become very, very busy. I don't have time to play with my children. Yet when they ask me to do something for them, I find myself unable to refuse, no matter how burdensome I find their demands. Their voices sound loud and shrill. My house looks unbearably messy, and I feel powerless to do anything about it. I say to myself: *I don't have time for this! I have too much to do!* I say: *I have to take care of everybody and nobody's taking care of me!* I sleep less and less and feel more and more tired. My hands shake and I crave sweets. I feel empty, hollow, and my edges seem to lose their firmness, as if I'm turning into a gas and my molecules are dispersing into an atmosphere too thin to support life. And then the memory comes.

Before I knew my father had molested me, the feelings cycled endlessly and attached themselves to the world outside my skin: If only my children weren't so demanding, I would think, I wouldn't feel so crazy.

Later, when I did know what had happened to me, still I would fail to recognize the aura. When the memories came they would take me by surprise. It was a long time before I connected the memories to the desperation that preceded them, and longer still before I knew, when I started to feel that desperate panic, that a memory was coming to the surface.

I thought I knew when he started to abuse me—I thought it was that day in November when I was three. But then I began to wonder: Why would he wait until then? If, as I heard him say, he was already doing it to my sister when she was a little girl, why would he wait to start with me? No use to say "My father wouldn't do that to me."

I thought I knew when he stopped—I thought the abuse ended with the enema he gave me the night after I slept with my boyfriend, when I was eighteen. But I can't be sure.

I will never know how often he did it. I tried to figure it out: They got drunk and quarreled almost every week at least once, sometimes two or three times. Did he do it to me every time that happened? I don't know. If he started when I was three, if he stopped when I was eighteen, that's fifteen years. Did it happen once a month? Twice a week? I don't know. It could have been a hundred times. It could have been a thousand.

TELLING

"I have to tell you something,"
I said to my husband one morning as soon as he was awake. I
told him about the enema my father had given me when I was
eighteen—twenty-seven years before this misty Saturday morning.

I hadn't told my husband about the experience before because it hadn't seemed important. I thought of it, when I
thought of it, as "odd," but that was all. My realization that my
father had molested me would come several months later. But
lately I had been talking with Kris about my relationship with
my father, and I had been having terrifying dreams about sexual

abuse. This morning I had startled awake with the sudden conviction that the enema was far more sinister, and shameful, than I had ever allowed myself to see.

"I'll understand if you find me disgusting," I told my husband. "But please tell me how you feel, because I don't think I can stand it if you feel disgusted and pretend you're not."

He held me close. "You're not disgusting. I love you." He paused. "I always knew he was a shit."

A few days later I told Kris. She regarded me with unruffled calm. I said, "I thought you'd say 'You did *that?* Get out of this office!'

"How awful for you to think I would react that way," she said, and she was right. It did feel awful.

Of course, I told myself, that incident wasn't really incest. Incest, I had read in Diana Russell's book *The Secret Trauma*, was "unwanted sexual contact with an older relative before the age of eighteen." I was eighteen, and I had asked for it, and it wasn't even really sexual contact, because he was a doctor. Besides, it couldn't have been incest, because my father wouldn't do that. He had done nothing wrong: I had.

It took more than a year in therapy before I was able to change this perception. Meanwhile I was beginning to realize that indeed my father would do, and had done, "that," had sexually abused me on many more occasions than I originally thought. I told my husband everything that came up. It seemed incredible to him that any father would molest his daughter; but he understood from the first that my father was capable of such a thing if anyone was. He believed me, and when I was overwhelmed with shame, sobbing and screaming, "I'm dirty and disgusting!" he held me tight and kept on telling me how much he loved me.

It was months before I could bring myself to tell anyone else that my father had molested me. The person I told first was a woman I'd gotten to know when our sons were best friends in nursery school. She had been through a terrible divorce, and I had cried with her and cursed her husband with her, and witnessed her magnificent efforts to make a safe, loving home for her three children. I trusted her completely; but even so I had to tell her on the phone because I didn't want to have to see her turn away from me.

"I thought there might be something like that," she said softly.

"I was afraid you'd think I'm disgusting," I said.

"I love you," she said, "and I think you're really special."

As I told more people, telling became a reliable way I could make myself feel better. People did not turn away from me in disgust; they loved me and supported me and expressed their rage at my father at a time when I found it almost impossible to love myself or express my own anger.

I know that I've been incredibly lucky. I've heard and read so many stories about women who were not believed, or were treated as if they'd made an embarrassing faux pas, or were admonished to forgive their abusers and forget the past.

My therapist suggested I join a group for incest survivors. It helped me to hear how the other women's stories resembled my own, even when the details were very different; and it helped me to see how we were all struggling with the consequences of what had happened to us. Over and over again I was struck by their courage—and my own. It became possible to say some things I had been unable to say to anyone except my therapist and my husband. After I said them in the group I could say them outside of the group, pushing at the edges of my shame until only a vestige remained. "There's a word I can't say," I said in group one night. I kept my eyes down, staring at the center of the rug. Everyone was quiet. "The word is *clitoris*," I said as tears came to my eyes and my face burned.

"There now," said Joyce Ann, one of the group leaders, in her exquisitely soft southern accent, "that wasn't so bad, was it?" It was bad, all right. But not as bad as I thought it would be.

As I began to assimilate what had happened to me I felt more and more that I wanted to tell my mother. Like my parents' drinking, the incest was a secret. It was a secret because my father wanted it to be a secret, but by speaking of it to my mother, I would be demonstrating that I didn't have to do what he wanted anymore, ever again.

In the spring of 1988, about nine months after the arrival of the box of letters, I wrote to my mother and asked her if she'd go to a family therapist with me—two two-hour sessions, one on Saturday and one on Sunday.

I didn't tell her what I wanted to talk about. I was afraid if I told her ahead of time she would refuse to come. I didn't want to be robbed of my opportunity to say everything I had to say, and I didn't want her to be alone when she found out. Lynn, the family therapist recommended by Kris, had done a lot of work with both incest survivors and their parents. I knew she would support my mother and encourage her to get some help when she went back to California.

My mother arrived on a Thursday. We got through Thursday night and Friday and drove to Lynn's house on Saturday. I could hardly breathe; my mother chatted about operas and movies she had been to recently.

I had written her a letter to read in therapy, because I was afraid I would lose my nerve and forget what I wanted to say. I wanted the letter to be perfect, as powerful and accurate as a piece submitted for publication. I could not imagine what my mother's response might be.

At the therapist's house my mother and I sat side by side on a long, soft sofa; Lynn sat on another sofa facing us across an Indian rug. Sun streamed through the tall windows. Lynn and my mother talked about the practice of therapy, and then Lynn said, "Betsy has written a letter she wants to read to you."

I took out the letter and held it in shaking hands. I turned to face my mother and began to read. "I want to tell you that Daddy molested me, and he molested Pat." I glanced up.

She kept looking at me. Her expression did not change. Her eyes were big behind her glasses.

"Did you know?" I whispered.

She shook her head. "No," she whispered back.

I went on reading. "It began when I was three and went on until I was eighteen . . ."

I finished, and waited for her response. She started talking about her own childhood.

"How do you feel about what your mother is saying?" Lynn said.

"She's talking about herself. I want to hear how she feels about what happened to *me*!"

It turned out that I had a hidden agenda, hidden even from myself. I thought all I wanted was to tell the secret, and get some information about things that happened in the family before I was born or that were concealed from me. But I realized that I was looking for a particular response from my mother. I wanted her to say she was sorry I had been abused. I wanted her to say she was sorry she had been so cold and distant when I was growing up, and sorry she had been drunk so often. She did not say this, until later in the session when, in tears, I asked her: "Aren't you sorry?"

"Of course I'm sorry!" she said. But I wanted her to offer it without being asked. I wanted to see that she was moved by the way I was violated by my father.

I wanted her to say, "Tell me how it was for you; I really want to know." I wanted her to undo what was done, her part of what was done when she did not ask what was happening to my sister and me, when she did not see.

I wanted her to tell me how adorable I was when I was little, how cute and funny and delightful. I wanted her to reach out to me, to put her arms around me. But later in the session, when she did put out her hand, I screamed at her: "Don't touch me! Don't touch me!"

I screamed and raved, and my mother listened with an impassive face, and I screamed some more, and then I said to Lynn: "Did I go too far?"

"No," she said. "I would have told you if you did."

That night my mother stayed home while the rest of us went to a movie. I was sure we would come back and find her dead, but in fact we found her in the kitchen making a peanut butter sandwich.

I felt so desperately sorry for her, sorry she had been cheated by my father, sorry she had cheated herself of being close to me when I was a child. But I couldn't touch her, or let her touch me. I was afraid that if I did, I'd have to take care of her and put aside my own need to be heard. I didn't want to be her mommy.

The second session went on for three hours instead of two, until we were all exhausted. I never got what I wanted. Lynn said there was no response I could get from my mother that would satisfy me, I was so angry with her.

My mother came to therapy with me when I asked her to. She believed what I told her, "because Betsy wouldn't lie," she told Lynn. In the therapy sessions and afterwards she tried to answer every question I asked her as completely as she could. She received my anger and did not try to retaliate. I asked her to see a therapist in California who had experience dealing with incest, and she did. I asked her to pay for some extra therapy for me, and she did. She gave me everything I asked for.

When I told my mother I was writing this book, she asked me to think very carefully about my decision to use my own name. A few months later she called to tell me she had thought it over, and she had no objection. "I don't believe there will be anything in this book to damage me," she said.

More months passed. I asked her if she would go with me to see the people whose condolence letters appear in this book, if she would ask them to give me permission to use their letters. She said she would go with me. She said she would not ask them, because she didn't know what was in the book. She did not ask (and has not ever asked) what was in the book. I said, "Is there anything you want to ask me about?"

She was silent for a moment, and then she said, "No."

We prepared ourselves to tell our children. We talked about it for weeks; it was hard for us to talk with them about sex in general, and we knew that telling them I had been sexually abused would be much harder. We felt deep sadness and horror that they should have to know that such things go on in the world. We wished we could protect them from this knowledge. But we also felt strongly that this should not be, must not be, a taboo subject. What if one of them were sexually abused? And surely they had friends who were being molested—some studies suggest that as many as one in five adults was sexually abused as a child. If it could happen to them, if it could happen to their friends, then it had to be talked about—otherwise how could they tell us, if it happened to them? Besides, they knew how upset I had been. They had seen me crying; they had experienced my anger, which, though it belonged to my parents, often got dumped on them. I had already told them I was remembering bad things that had happened to me when I was a child; but we wanted them to know what had happened to me, and what was happening now. We wanted to help them understand that my distress had nothing to do with them.

And so, four months after I told my mother, we started reading a sex education book to our sons, a chapter a night. They were ten and twelve. We read the book because we wanted them to have all the information it contained, but in particular we wanted to read them the chapter on sex crimes. Even after all the work I'd done, the phrase surprised me: sex crimes. What my father did to me was a crime. He could have been arrested and put in jail for it.

We read the chapter. I said, "Fellas, there's something we want to tell you. What the book said about parents forcing their children to have sex with them—that happened to me. My father did that when I was growing up. That's what I've been working on in therapy, and it's why I've been crying so much and acting so mad sometimes."

They were silent. "What he did was evil and wicked," I said, "but it's not something you can't talk about. If anything like that ever happened to you, we'd want you to be able to tell us about it, just like we're telling you about this."

My husband said, "I want you to know how brave Mommy is. She's been working really hard, and she's been doing a wonderful job of dealing with this."

William said, "Can we watch TV now?" and they disappeared. For the rest of the evening they hugged me a lot.

From time to time my husband and I refer to the abuse, always in general terms. My sons know about this book, and have mentioned it to their friends. When they see me crying or raging—it happens less often these days—I'm careful to remind them where the feelings are coming from. They show no signs of having been damaged by the information we gave them. As for me, being able to tell them made me feel clean.

CONNECTIONS

The day Tom had three teeth pulled, William said, "Smile so I can look in your mouth."

"I don't feel like it."

"Oh, come on," said William.

"I don't feel like it."

"WHAT'S YOUR PROBLEM?" William yelled.

Tom picked up a wooden chair and threw it on the slate floor, and then threw himself onto the sofa, crying.

I was furious with William—and furious at my father for all

the times I had to do what he wanted even when it hurt, or risk his anger and everything that came with it.

Tom had his teeth pulled early in the summer that incest memories were coming up faster than I could process them. In a few weeks my mother would arrive for the sessions we had planned with a family therapist. I had told my sons that I had been having painful memories of my father, but I had not yet told them what those memories were about. I was full of rage, and didn't know what to do with it.

William came into the kitchen and tried to catch my eye. I wouldn't look at him. "What are you so mad about?" he asked.

"It hurts where he had his teeth pulled, and you won't leave him alone," I said.

"It hurts me just as bad when I have my retainer tightened," he said. "And he comes in my room and he takes my stuff and he turns off the TV when I'm watching, and you never do anything. You never get mad at *him* when he does stuff to *me*."

I felt the hair rising on the back of my neck, and my hands began to shake, and I picked up a plastic tumbler and threw it on the floor as hard as I could. It smashed into splinters. William stared at me. I made my voice cold and hard. "Why don't you just go punch him in the jaw and pay him back for all the rotten things he ever did to you!"

"I don't believe this!" William was yelling and crying at the same time. "*He* threw the chair, and you're mad at *me*!" He ran upstairs to his room and slammed the door.

When my father came home from work my parents would have a few drinks while they fixed dinner together. Then we would eat, a lively, chatty meal, the best part of the day. The crabby hangover was over, and so was the tension that had built up before the day's first drink, and the drunken battle was yet to come.

Dinner was often late, and afterwards they would leave the dishes and go on drinking wine. I would go to bed. And then from my room upstairs I would hear them start. My father's murmuring whine: "What's the matter, honey?" My mother's cold reply: "You know." What were those fights about? I can't remember, but I must have known, because I do remember thinking that the issues were stupid, not worth fighting over.

There would be more murmurs, more coldness, and then it would start to heat up. She would pick and pick, her voice mean and shrill, and he would answer in a soft whine. She would cry, and he would murmur. She would attack, and he would defend. He would begin to get angry, his control would begin to slip, and she would press her advantage.

Twice when I was a teenager I saw bruises on my mother's face. The first time my father told me, privately, that she had fallen down while dancing in the living room. Drunk: He did not say it, but I assumed it. The other time he told me, in her presence, that she had jumped out of the car while he was driving. She shot him a venomous look, which meant, I thought, that she wanted me to believe he had hit her. It never occurred to me that he did hit her; as far as I knew he never had. What he did do was touch me in the dark.

A little while after I broke the plastic tumbler, William came downstairs and we all apologized to one another. I went on fixing Jell-O and Instant Breakfast for Tom's dinner—the dentist had forbidden solid food for the rest of the day. Tom said, "Can I stay home from camp tomorrow?"

"No." For years I could not say no to my children. I held the line on junk food and television for a while, and on riding without seat belts always. But otherwise I gave them pretty much whatever they asked for, however inconvenient or expensive. When I didn't, we would fight, and that scared me. I was afraid of their anger, and of my own. By this time I could sometimes manage it, but it terrified me.

"Will you pick me up early and take me to get some corn dogs?"

"No." My anxiety was building.

"Will you take me tonight to get some?"

"No." I felt I would explode.

"Why not?" he screamed. "You said you'd get me some meat, you stupid asshole!" He threw his shoe against the wall and William faded back up to his room.

And suddenly I was *so mad*. My stomach hurt. I was *so mad* about all the times I wanted to say no to my father but was too afraid of his anger. Everybody who knew him talked about how calm he was, but his friends and acquaintances never saw him lose control. Sometimes—the first time when I was three or four, the last time when I was nine or ten—he would get mad and grab me and drag me to the bottom of the stairs. He would sit on the stairs and turn me over his knee and pull my pants down and spank my bare bottom over and over and over. Once when he reached for me I got away and ran to my room and locked myself in. But he came after me and beat on the door and shouted, "Open the door or I'll break it down." I lay on the rumpled jacquard bedspread on my low bed, looking up at the spots on the ceiling and listening to the sound of his fists on the door. I was afraid to open the door but more afraid not to, afraid of what he would do to me if he had to break it to get to me. I opened the door. And he spanked me, leaving the skin on my bottom as hot and red as if it were sunburned.

I had to do what he wanted. I had to stand beside him at the kitchen counter and watch while he gave me salad-making lessons: Rub the wooden bowl with a cut garlic clove, tear (don't cut) the lettuce into bite-size pieces, pour a little oil over them, and "toss it till it shines." I wasn't allowed to do it, only to watch and listen to the lecture.

When I was in high school, an invitation to join a social club was offered and then withdrawn after one of the members blackballed me. They called my mother and asked her to tell me, and she did. I sat in the living room and cried. "I feel so ashamed," I sobbed.

"Come and sit on my lap," my father said. I shook my head. "Come and sit on my lap," he repeated, and I had to go and sit on his lap and pretend to be comforted.

I had to let him spank me and I had to take salad-making lessons and I had to sit on his lap; and at night in my bed I had to let him touch me. It didn't matter what I wanted. I knew there would be consequences if I tried to refuse. He would do to me what he had done to my sister: He would pay me back for all the rotten things anybody ever did to him. The iron hand in the velvet glove would get me.

So I did what he wanted, and ate my anger. When I was grown up, with children of my own, I found myself unable to set limits, just as I had been unable to set limits as a child; I did what my children wanted, just as I had done what my father wanted. But because they were so much less powerful than he, I did not have to keep swallowing my anger. Often I spit it out, screaming and ranting at them, making them pay the price for what he did.

I did not know that was what I was doing. I only knew I was angry with them and they didn't deserve it. Until I had gotten back the missing pieces of my past, I couldn't make the connection between my anger at my children in the present and the numb compliance of my childhood. And the first time I did make that connection—on the very day Tom's teeth were pulled—my anger got much worse.

"You're starving me to death!" Tom yelled, after I told him once again that the dentist had forbidden solid food until the next morning.

"You won't die," I said, quite calmly. "You might get very hungry, but you'll live through it."

He screamed and threw a newspaper in my face, and my calm deserted me. I screamed and screamed, like a two-year-old having a tantrum; I ran back and forth going, "EEK! EEEK! EEEEEEK!" Then I found some words, and screamed them: "I AM SO ANGRY! YOU THREW A NEWSPAPER IN MY FACE JUST BECAUSE I WOULDN'T GIVE YOU WHAT YOU WANTED! I AM JUST FURIOUS!"

I can't remember having tantrums as a child.

I went upstairs to my room and started working on the bookkeeping, hoping to lose myself in columns and rows. Tom followed me and lay down on my bed and demanded meat.

I was calm once more. I said, calmly, "Sometimes it happens that you have to be uncomfortable for a while."

"Shithead!" he yelled, and threw my pillow on the floor.

"EEEK!" I screamed, and then I cleared my throat and said, in a loud voice, "When you call me names I get mad, and then I scream." I demonstrated: "EEEK!"

"Idiot!" he yelled.

I got up from my desk and ran over to the bed and stood over him, yelling, "You're in my space. Get out of my space! Get out! Get out!"

But he wouldn't leave the room; so I did.

I was enraged—with my father, who invaded my space and didn't care, didn't even notice that I didn't want him there.

I stormed about in the kitchen, and then I stomped up the

stairs to my room, where I found Tom still lying on my bed. "I'm going to buy milk," I told him.

"I'm coming!" he yelled. I got in my car and unlocked the front door for him on the passenger side, but he pulled on the handle of the back door and glared at me through the window. I opened the back door and he got in. "Turn off the radio," he said.

"No, I like this song," I said.

"Turn off the radio," he said, in a voice full of escalating rage.

"No!" I yelled, and backed out of the driveway.

"Turn off the radio."

"No! No! No!" I drove back into the driveway and turned off the motor. "It's not safe for me to drive now," I said, and got out of the car, leaving him there. I removed myself from the scene.

Upstairs, I knocked on William's door, and he opened it. "In case you heard all the screaming, I just wanted you to know that I didn't break anything and I didn't hurt anybody." He gave me a hug.

As a child I couldn't remove myself from the scene. My father held me down. I knew I couldn't get away, and even if I could run from him, I knew he'd catch me, and if I resisted he might . . . do what he did to my sister. Stick that big, long, hard thing like a baseball bat into that hole that goes way up deep into the inside of me.

She cried when he did it to her. I could hear her, from my crib across the room, when she was fourteen and I was three. "It hurts. It hurts. Don't. Please don't. It hurts." She sounded like a little animal. He paid her back for all the rotten things anybody ever did to him.

95

In later years he would pull the dog's ears, and Lucky—a smooth, shiny little black mongrel, good-natured and silly—would squeal, and I would yell as loud as I could: "STOP PULL-ING LUCKY'S EARS!" But he wouldn't stop. My mother and my sister would stand there watching, silently, and my father would smile and say, "He likes it."

Tom came into the house and sat down at the kitchen table. I leaned over and put my arms around him. "All this screaming is pretty awful for you, isn't it?"

He nodded.

"But you know it doesn't have much to do with you. You know who I'm really mad at."

"Grandpa."

"Yep."

"You don't have to take it out on me. It's not fair."

"No, it's not fair at all. It must be horrible to have me yelling and screaming at you, especially when you just had your teeth pulled and you hurt and you can't have anything good to eat."

I hugged him and he leaned against me for a minute. Then he jumped up, grinning, his eyes wide with delight. "I know what I can eat! Peanut butter! Only I don't want that natural stuff. I mean, that's okay, I can eat it, but what I really want is Jif. Will you take me to get some?"

Yes.

Mother and Daddy, Pat and me, 1944

My father and his mother, 1912

My mother as a child

Five generations: my mother,
her great grandmother, her
grandmother, Aunt Gertrude,
and Pat, 1935

Pat in her early
thirties

My father's
favorite picture
of me: age 16,
1958

My father in
his army uniform:
the picture I
carried around
with me while he
was overseas, 1944

Pat in our parents'
San Francisco
apartment

Photo taken of me in the backyard
by my father, age about 7

HISTORY

The last time I saw my mother's father I was twenty-eight and he was eighty, and dying of emphysema. He was shorter than I remembered, shorter than me in fact, and very thin. He sat at his kitchen table with a cigarette in one hand and a glass of whiskey in the other. His hands shook when he raised the glass to his lips, and he could hardly drink it, he was coughing so hard. When we left, my mother and father and I smiled ghastly smiles and pretended there was nothing the matter, and I said, "I'll see you in October"—this was July—and I knew, and knew that he knew, that we would never see each other again. That night my mother sat on the floor in front of the fire with a glass of wine and the bottle within reach, and she cried and said to my father: "Give me something so it won't feel so bad," and my father said, "There's nothing you can take for that."

By then I knew that my mother's earliest memory was of separating from her father, though that was not how she characterized it. I had asked her: "What's the first thing you remember?" And what she remembered was walking through a light snowfall and getting into a stagecoach with her mother. Her voice as she told me was calm, contemplative. Where were they going? I asked her. Back to Oakland, she said, to live with Grandma. They were leaving her father.

She was three years old; I understood, hearing this story, that her world was being torn apart and she didn't know why. But what she conveyed to me was the scene, the crisp feeling of the snowy air, the stagecoach waiting on the empty road. And she told me that much only because I asked.

My mother did not talk about her father when I was a child; she did not tell me until I was grown how her grandmother used to say, "Your father doesn't care about you—that's why he never comes to see you." Her father's version, she added, was that her grandmother hated him and wouldn't let him visit.

I remember as a child seeing my mother cry when her father failed to show up for a family party, and I remember understanding, though I don't believe my mother actually said so, that he could not be depended upon.

There was one story about him my mother used to tell me, about the night she was spotted in a speakeasy by a friend of her father's when she was a teenager. "Bax," said the friend to my grandfather later, "have you got a daughter?"

"Yes I do," my grandfather replied, "but how did you know?"

"Because I saw a jane in a joint in Hayward, and she looked just like you!"

My mother didn't tell me why this story was important to her, but I hear it now as a story about being connected to her father. Although she had not lived with him since she was three, she had something of his: his face. And the story ended with his telling her to stay out of speakeasies. Maybe that meant—maybe she hoped that meant—that he cared about her.

She did not speak to me of her mother, who died when she was six. I knew she had been raised by her grandmother. I knew that her grandmother loved baseball and the opera, and took my mother to both with equal enthusiasm. My mother hung on to that, I think, as an emblem of the happy childhood she wished she had had.

I knew the household also included Grandpa, Great-Grandma, and the aunt and uncle my mother always referred to as "my crazy Aunt Gertrude" and "my crazy Uncle Julius." I thought of this aunt and uncle as lovable eccentrics, like the characters in a funny play. My sister lived with my mother's family, too, and my father loved to tell how Julius taught her all his curses and obscenities before she was four. The day my mother took my father to meet her family, "we were greeted at the gate by Pat, then almost four," he wrote in his *Letter to Betsy*. "The face of an angel and the vocabulary of a stevedore. 'Hello, you old son of a bitch,' she greeted me, timidly. Julius was responsible."

I did not know until I was grown that Gertrude and Julius were child molesters. My mother told me they had abused at least two young girls before my sister was born. My father did know that about them. But he wrote in his *Letter to Betsy* that Julius was "a most remarkable man. He was Belgian, born in

Paris, with a gypsy grandmother. He spoke a great variety of languages including at least one Chinese dialect. He had been all over the world. . . ." And so on, sentence after sentence portraying Julius as a prototypical counterculture hero.

Did Julius and Gertrude initiate my sister, preparing the way for my father? Was that the real source of my father's admiration, that he and Julius belonged to the same secret society?

Both my parents grew up poor, though this was not spoken of during my childhood. In the first chapter of his *Letter to Betsy*, my father lovingly described his family's early, and brief, prosperity, and the bank in Greenwood, Mississippi, where his father worked at the time: a place where "money could be plainly seen."

My paternal grandfather had gotten a degree in business from the University of Mississippi, had done graduate work in banking at a school in New York, and at the bank in Greenwood was promoted to cashier and given an office of his own. Then he turned to farming. He farmed cotton three years running, in three different locations. The first place my father remembered as exotic and beautiful, with woods to explore, good fishing, plentiful game, and a set of Poe's works in the house. The second year they lived in a ramshackle house with no electricity, water from a pump over the horse trough, and an open-backed privy infested with wasp nests. The third year my father and his mother and sister stayed in town while my grandfather worked on yet another farm. The fourth year the family moved to Jackson, and my grandfather got a job as a bookkeeper for his brother-in-law, who became one of the richest and most powerful men in the state. "We rented a tiny house that was miserably cold and empty all day," my father wrote. "It was always dirty. The food was terrible. We were poor." His mother also worked, first in an insurance company and later, until she retired in her sixties, in a bank. My father wrote that his parents arrived home "late and out of sorts," and that as the years passed, his mother would never speak of the farming years except to say, "That's when we lost all we had."

I think of my grandmother as tight-lipped and rageful, making her husband pay and pay for his failure; and of my grandfather as rageful in turn, but venting his frustration slyly in the practical jokes for which he was famous. One of my father's favorite stories about him concerned the time my sister's fiancé visited my grandfather and was offered a piece of sugarcane to chew. You were supposed to swallow the juice and spit out the fiber, but Nate, a city boy from Chicago, didn't know that. Eager to make a good impression on his fiancée's family, he chewed up the cane as best he could and swallowed it. "Have some more sugarcane," my grandfather said. Nate took some more, chewed and swallowed. "Have some more sugarcane," my grandfather said again. My father ended this story, which he told often, by laughing heartily about how sick the cane fiber made Nate.

Yet in my father's autobiography he characterized his father not as cruel but as brave. "His greatest virtue was courage. . . . Somehow he never gave up and never complained. He kept his problems to himself."

Nor did my father venture to criticize his mother in the official version of his childhood. "My mother has many faults, as who doesn't," he wrote. "To elaborate on them would serve no purpose. On the positive side, she had a fierce dedication to her children and made enormous sacrifices to help us through school."

For me, two stories characterize my father's relationship with his mother. He never told the first story himself; it was told to me by my mother after he died, a story about the day he came home from high school, thrilled with the lecture he had just heard on evolution. He was eager to share his excitement with his mother—and she made him kneel beside her and pray aloud for forgiveness.

The other story does appear in his *Letter to Betsy*, and I heard him tell it many times when I was growing up. My grandmother was a devout Southern Baptist, a regular churchgoer and a lifelong teetotaler. Once while she was visiting us she complained of indigestion. My father poured her a little glass of crème de menthe, and, as he told the story, "it did the trick."

"This doesn't have any alcohol in it, does it?" she asked, and my father assured her that it did not. He had taken the precaution of drawing a decimal point in front of the legend "60 proof" on the bottle. Prohibition had never been repealed in Mississippi, and after my grandmother got home she reported that she had asked for crème de menthe in the stores but nobody had it. So my father wrote to a friend and asked him to get some crème de menthe from the bootlegger—and to be sure to put a decimal point on the bottle where it said "60 proof."

I met a couple at a party once; they had a pet pig which they forced, when it misbehaved, to eat bacon. My father would have loved that story. Its point is violation, and so is the point of the crème de menthe story. So, too, is the point of the evolution story: My father's mother was able to violate him spiritually even in adolescence, when a child's energy for breaking away reaches its peak.

Did my father's mother violate him sexually as well as spiritually and psychologically? Did his father vent his rage not only in cruel jokes but also upon the bodies of his children? I can only guess; but I can't help thinking there is a connection between these stories and my father's professed sexual values. "The comedy of life has seduction as its central theme," he wrote. "Throughout the animal kingdom, and man is an animal, the stage for sex is set by the female. . . . I seriously doubt whether any amount of courtship on the part of a man would inspire any degree of passion in a woman unless she were already receptive. . . . So the comedy proceeds to the particular end desired by the woman. . . . Any assumption of a dominant pose by the man is ridiculous." A bizarre statement from a child raper, but one that reveals my father's perception of himself—and perhaps of his father as well—as the helpless victim of manipulation by females.

My father's account of his own career seems to parallel his description of his father's, though my grandfather went bankrupt and my father was a financial and professional success. Yet both father and son, in the son's mind, experienced early promise followed by disillusionment. In my father's autobiography he wrote with passionate nostalgia about his arrival in San Francisco in 1935:

The train reached the Oakland Mole at midnight, and I boarded the ferry, suddenly cool for the first time in days. Impatient for a glimpse of the city, I stood outside on the front deck. The cold wind cut through my linen suit and I held my straw hat. I shivered with the cold but even more with excitement. I never suspected that I was beginning a whole new life with a new cast of characters, new values, new objectives. Least of all did I expect to find your mother somehow waiting with a new soul for me, a soul as fresh as the cold clean air I was breathing there in the center of the bay.

In San Francisco my father did seven years of postgraduate work in surgery, and then joined the army. For most of the war he was stationed at Letterman Hospital in San Francisco; in 1945 he spent six months on Okinawa, where he operated on wounded combat soldiers.

When he came back, he perceived himself as somehow un-manned by his army service. A month or so passed before he got a one-year appointment to head the surgical service and training program at Southern Pacific Hospital. A hoped-for teaching appointment at the University of California "did not materialize," as he put it, and he did not pursue it, although people said he had a talent for teaching and he said he loved it. Instead he moved to the suburbs and entered private practice with a group of men he mostly disliked, accepting compensation he considered insufficient. He became successful, respected, be-loved by his patients and colleagues; he reaped many honors. But there is nothing about all that in his autobiography, except for a passing reference to the "hate, fear, and guilt" generated by the money quarrels of his partners. Nothing about the prac-tice of surgery itself, and almost nothing about my mother, though he did write that she wanted to stay in our flat, lower-middle-class neighborhood instead of moving, as he wanted to do and we eventually did, to Hillsborough, the most prestigious community in Northern California.

His return from overseas, at the age of thirty-four, appears on page 180 of his autobiography; the book ends on page 193 with his account of putting me aboard the plane for my fresh-man year in college, when he was forty-eight. Fourteen years in thirteen pages. Most of what he wrote concerns my sister and me and our romantic conquests: I think he saw us, and meant for us to see ourselves, acting in a play he wrote, in roles he trained us for, on a stage he set, in a drama he directed.

In that last, abbreviated chapter he presents himself as an almost tragic figure musing on his lost potential and aborted dreams, in contrast to the energy and commitment he saw him-self bringing to San Francisco when he first arrived there. But that is his official version. I wonder, did that energy and com-mitment ever exist apart from his romantic fantasy? I can't forget—I won't let myself forget—that by 1969, when he wrote so poignantly in his autobiography about my mother waiting in San Francisco with a new soul for him, he had betrayed her over and over, with other women and with his daughters.

Why? Why did he betray her, and us? Why did she refuse to see it happening? Should I settle for the pat, tidy, deterministic view? She abandoned us because she was abandoned; he violated us because he was violated. No. They made choices. They were responsible for what they did: not their parents, though their parents should have loved and cared for them and didn't.

In his *Letter to Betsy* my father told the story of a party at the officers' club during the war. "That party was the night I pinched one of the wives as she talked to the visiting general, a real prissy woman with great ambitions for her husband. I knew she couldn't give a sign of it, so a little later I pinched her twice as hard. Then I was ashamed. She was still exchanging polite nonsense with the general but with a great big tear in the corner of her eye."

He recognized this woman as a victim, a victim like the child I was and my sister was: "I knew she couldn't give a sign of it." He violated her—in a small, trivial way, perhaps, compared to what he did to us, but it was a violation nevertheless. And then he did it again. And then he was ashamed. What did that shame mean? It meant he understood her humiliation. He knew what he was doing. And then he held the story close to him for twenty-five years, and then he wrote it down for his daughter to read.

I want to go back in time to that party, and stand beside that woman, my fellow victim, and say to my father: "Take your hands off her, you daughter fucker, or I'll cut your balls off!" I want to make a scene in the officers' club. I want to shout it out for everyone to hear. I want everyone to know what he did to her, what he did to my mother, what he did to my sister, what he did to me. And why. He did it because he wanted to, to make himself feel powerful.

"MY OWN PRECIOUS BOY"

Two days before his seventeenth birthday my father left his home in Jackson and went to Oxford, Mississippi, to begin his freshman year at Ole Miss. His mother wrote him this letter the day after he left.

September 14, 1928

My own precious boy:

Here it has only been twenty-four hours since you left me, and I feel like it has been forever except I have all the memories of the love and sweet thoughtfulness to go over every spare minute. I thought I could not

107

bear to go home yesterday, but of course had to go to [your] Sister. It just broke my heart to go into your room. I do not know when I will even go in there to straighten up. This morning when my eyes flew open the first thing I thought was that it was time for you to go to the bathroom, and then I remembered. But Mother is making this sacrifice for you to be educated, and of course there is no grief so great that God cannot heal. I'll always miss you and long for you, but this terrible ache and void in my life will become softened, and I will be able to rejoice in all the good things that will come your way for I know there will not be a boy there who can stand any higher in any way than you can. There is not a better brain in any boy's head than in yours, and I know you are going to stand right at the top of everything. Am anxious to hear how the Professors are going to like you and how everything goes.

I had a letter from the Scouts yesterday inviting me to the party tonight. On the bottom was a postscript written by Mr. Morgan saying how he admires you and how he will miss you, and urging that I come, but I could not go without my boy. There would be no joy in it for me.

And when you get this my little baby boy will be seventeen. This is the first birthday in your whole life that I have not been able to take you in my arms and kiss you for each year. My heart will be with you and I will be sending you more than that many kisses by wireless. Tune your heart in and get my message. I could not afford to buy you a fine present but in your Gladstone bag there is a little love gift for the dearest boy a mother ever had.

It is time for the bank to open so I must stop.

Hearts and hearts full of love and worlds of kisses and good wishes for my seventeen year old boy.

Devotedly yours,
Mother

MONEY

One morning at breakfast when I was six or seven, my sister reported that she had passed my room on the way to the bathroom in the middle of the night and found me crouching on the floor, naked, peering into my money jar.

"Are you all right?" she had asked me.

"There's something funny about my money jar," I said. But I had no memory of the incident when she told me about it the next morning. When I checked my money jar, it looked the same. Nothing seemed to be missing. Only looking back can I see that of course something *was* missing, something *had* been stolen from me—power, integrity, autonomy—and begin to appreciate the crushing symbolic weight that money had and still has for me.

I hoarded the allowance they gave me. I collected coin banks, and I remember one in particular that I ordered from the Johnson and Smith novelty catalog. I had yearned for it; I was sure it was going to change my life. It was red enameled steel, about the size of a cigar box, with six slots and six oval windows behind which labels could be placed. The slots gave access to six small boxes within. You identified your six goals, divided your income into six parts, and inserted them into the six slots to be stored in the six boxes until you had enough to buy your heart's six desires.

The red box locked with a tiny key, like the key to a diary. I loved it, but I was foiled by my own inability to think of six things, or even one, that I wanted. I wanted the money more than I wanted any thing: to have it in my control. Its potential was limitless, as long as it remained unspent. So I didn't keep my money in the red box; I kept it in a peanut butter jar, and watched it accumulate. We had a charge account at the corner grocery, where I stopped every day on my way home from school and got Necco Wafers, and my mother gave me money on Saturday mornings to go to the movies or the roller skating rink. I didn't need to spend my money to buy things; I put it in my money jar instead, a hedge against future dangers and disasters. Saving it made me feel safe.

I learned what it was to wish for something when I was four or five. "Make a wish," a friend said. We were riding in the backseat of my parents' car.

"What do you mean?" I said.

"You know. Wish for something, something you want."

I waved the dandelion blossom I was holding. "I wish for this."

"No, no, you're supposed to wish for something you don't have."

I went through the motions, but it seemed an empty gesture. If I didn't have it—whatever it was—I didn't believe there was any way I could get it. Even now it is very hard for me to wish for something. I have preferred, for as long as I can remember, not to want anything, in case I might want something I can't get. Better to live as if in poverty, never letting myself know I want something, than to want something and not receive it.

In my family there were rules about giving and receiving, though they were never spoken or acknowledged. You could not ask for what you wanted. If someone asked you what you wanted, you could not say. You could not ask others what they wanted. And you had to like what you were given.

As it does in most families, a gift expressed the giver's perception of the receiver and the relationship between them. The difference was, in my family it had to express an ideal perception, and an ideal relationship, and it had to express them perfectly. You weren't supposed to make a mistake, and if you did, it meant something awful.

"Guess what song this is," my son Tom said recently, and played a few notes on his saxophone. He grinned. "If you can't guess, it means you don't love me."

I laughed so hard the dogs came trotting in to check on me. He had captured exactly the way it was when I was growing up. If I guessed wrong and gave my parents a disappointing gift, that meant I didn't love them. If my mother or father guessed wrong and gave me a gift that disappointed me, that meant she or he didn't love me. My sister had a talent for choosing gifts that people loved, and she always seemed sincerely to love what I, at least, gave her. But the rest of us, my mother, my father, and me, all pretended we loved any gift, whatever it was; the stakes were too high to tell the truth.

Perhaps it was the pretense that led me to mingle gift-giving in my mind with the other things that nobody talked about, the things that were happening in the dark, in secret. In the dark I learned that there was no such thing as giving, only having things taken from me; no such thing as receiving, only having things shoved down my throat. I learned not to want, because what I wanted had no importance: none. None at all.

One rule was suspended at Christmas. I was allowed to ask, out loud, for one thing I wanted. Once it was a stuffed lion with a big yellow mane. Another year it was a three-color ballpoint pen, and my parents joked with their friends about how easy I was to please. The year I was eleven I wanted a white knit top with a turtleneck and three-quarter-length sleeves. I described it to my parents, and to everyone who asked me what I wanted for Christmas, and I thought about it constantly. I saw myself with curly hair and without my glasses, standing in the center of a group of girls, wearing my white knit top. I was sure I knew which box under the Christmas tree contained it, and several times every day I'd pick it up and shake it, and hear it sliding softly back and forth.

But I had forgotten the petticoat my mother had bought me a few months earlier as a surprise. Those were the days when girls wore three or four petticoats under wide cotton dirndl skirts. I'd had my eye on one with a stiff, plain skirt gathered onto a yoke, though I hadn't told anyone what I wanted. The one my mother bought me had three tiers of graduated ruffles. I had let her see my disappointment, and she had let me know how hurt she was. And now, on Christmas morning, I opened the box and found an elastic cinch belt. "We decided not to get you clothes anymore," my mother said, "because you never like what we pick out."

There was little talk of money when I was growing up—so little that I thought of it as a subject, like death, that nice people did not discuss. I never heard my sister ask for cashmere sweaters, though her demands are part of Family History. She loved clothes, and must also have asked for dresses, skirts, shoes, lingerie, but there was something emblematic about the cashmere sweaters, possessed (we all believed) in large numbers by her high school classmates who lived in Hillsborough. My father wrote in his *Letter to Betsy* that she wanted "money, and the things money can buy." When my sister was a child, they told me, they couldn't afford to buy her the things they were able to buy for me later on. Because of some defect in her character— they did not say this but I understood that they believed it—she equated love with money, and felt deprived of one because she hadn't had the other. This—I understood that they believed it —was a willful error on her part, typical of her chronic ingratitude, since of course love had been lavished upon her, as it was upon me. My father referred disparagingly to her desire for "popularity, status, and material wealth," as if these desires were evidence of depravity. "She had a clear idea of what she wanted from very early in her teens," he wrote. "She had an iron will and never deviated one degree from her course." He was not surprised when she divorced her husband to marry a millionaire. "Max," he told me, as if he were confiding a shameful secret, "is so goddamn rich you wouldn't believe it."

113

. . .

My mother managed the money in our family, perhaps because my father found money so powerful, and so terrifying, he didn't want anything to do with it. I remember my mother paying the bills at a big oak table, one of the ugly pieces of furniture that came to us with our house and stayed with us until we left it. My father had covered the tabletop with a piece of linoleum, cream-colored with a paint-spatter pattern, the same linoleum they installed themselves on our kitchen floor when I was about five.

"Don't touch the linoleum cutter," he told me over and over while he did the job. It had a curved blade like the beak of a bird of prey, and I watched him cut the linoleum with beautiful smooth strokes, as if he were cutting through butter. He worked all day one Saturday, and left the knife on the floor.

Sunday morning I got up before they did, gently turned the knob of their bedroom door, found it locked, and knew that meant I was to tiptoe quietly away and amuse myself. I went downstairs and picked up the knife and a scrap of linoleum, ready to cut it straight and true, the way my daddy did, but the knife slipped and sliced across the forefinger of my left hand. I went to the bathroom and got a Band-Aid. The cut was almost as long as the Band-Aid; I put it on lengthwise over the cut, and blood leaked out around the edges. I heard my parents' door opening. They liked me to come and get in bed with them on Sunday mornings, but this morning I did not go until they called me. Then I went and stood beside their bed, my hand held behind me.

I knew they would be angry, and they were. But at least, my father said, I didn't need stitches. I still have the scar, a silvery line crossing my knuckle diagonally from left to right.

114

. . .

I don't want to be back there, standing in the doorway watching my mother paying bills at the oak table with the linoleum top, in dim light from the ceiling fixture that casts harsh shadows on her face and across the papers she works on. "Are you mad?" I ask from the doorway. "No!" she snaps, without looking up.

Now I manage the money in our family, and get angry when I pay the bills, and snap at my children when they interrupt me. What does money mean to me? Blood. Something you have to have to live, but it leaks away and you can't stop it, like the blood that leaked out of me when the linoleum knife cut me, and then every month starting when I was twelve. A bloody secret: You can't talk about it.

For a year before I got my first period I went to the bathroom a dozen times a day to see if I was bleeding. What if I bled on my clothes and it soaked through to the outside and people saw the stain on the back of my skirt? I remembered my sister's heavy periods. I remembered when we drove through the Midwest on a family vacation, how she begged my father to stop because she needed to change her pad; how he wouldn't stop until we arrived at the motel where we were spending the night; how she ran inside and hid in the bathroom. His covert rage, and her blood, are linked in my mind with something I witnessed on that vacation, something between my father and my sister that I can almost remember, but not quite.

When I finally got my period it was totally unexpected. I was playing with my friends in the backyard and I came in to go to the bathroom and saw the spot of blood, dark red and the size of a silver dollar. I seemed to feel a sudden change in air pressure, a silent thunderclap. I didn't want to tell my mother, but I needed her help to negotiate the unknown territory of belts and pads and blood that wouldn't stop flowing no matter how much you wanted it to.

She fixed me up with what I needed and called me "my little woman," and put me in her bed and covered me up and tiptoed out the door. I remember the way the pad felt between my legs—huge, intrusive—and I remember thinking: Now I'll have this every month for years and years and years, my whole life almost.

It meant I could get pregnant. How did you get pregnant? I had no idea. I studied the two books my mother had given me years earlier, *Growing Up to Be a Baby* and *Being Born*, but I couldn't understand the process from the authors' descriptions. Could you get pregnant if you got in the same bed with a man? If I got in bed with my parents on a Sunday morning, could I get pregnant? I went to my mother, intending to ask calmly for information, and found myself suddenly in tears and almost incoherent. "What's happening to me?" I sobbed. "I don't understand!" She answered the questions I was able to ask, though not the ones I couldn't bring myself to utter.

Blood and money, money and blood. When I sit down to pay the bills I feel like I'm bleeding; the money is bleeding away, a hemorrhage of money like a miscarriage. I don't spend much money on myself, but the bills keep coming all the same. I have to stop it, but I can't stop it; my insides are bleeding away and I can't tell anybody. After I've entered every transaction in the ledger, I'm going to find out that the money's all gone, it's all bled away, and it will be my fault, because I'm the one who pays the bills and does the bookkeeping. Without money my husband can't be a man. So I can't tell him. I can't even let myself find out. I can't ever catch up on the bookkeeping because the bottom line will destroy us. How much money have we got? It's a secret, and if it comes to light he'll die and I'll be left alone.

But I'm alone already, alone with this secret, carrying it around inside. I don't want to be alone with the secret any longer.

In fact, we have enough money, a circumstance which, miraculously, everybody else in the family takes for granted. But I feel poor. When my children ask me to buy them a yo-yo or give them a quarter for a video game, I feel violated. Their wanting overwhelms me: Buy me this, give me that, I want, I want, I want, and I have to give them what they want and I can't take care of myself until everyone else has gotten everything he wants, and they won't ever get everything they want, so I'll have to wait forever. I don't dare want anything, because all I can see ahead is endless frustration, forever and ever and ever, world without end.

I'm at Girl Scout camp, breathing the clean evergreen scent of the high Sierras, and two girls are giving me orders: "Go get firewood," says one, and the other, seeing me gathering wood, says, "What are you doing? Don't do that—go sweep up around the campfire." I have to do what they want. As I run back and forth between them, my face is impassive, until suddenly I run away and fling myself on my sleeping bag, the old army bag my father brought back from the Pacific after the war. I gasp and sob but no tears come. I can't get my breath, can't speak. The counselor comes and sits beside me, puts her hand on my back, and finally I calm down enough to tell her what happened. Her voice is soft: "You know, you don't have to do something just because somebody tells you to." I didn't know. Nobody has ever told me that before.

Grocery shopping with my children: Tom says, "Can I have some Doritos? Can I have some Pringles? Can I have a bag of Milky Ways? Can I have some Chips Ahoy?" Like the girls at camp, he wants something from me. William, hiding his own wishes even from himself, tries to make him stop asking, and it turns into a squabble between them, with me in the middle. I

117

cringe, holding on to the cart with white knuckles, saying no, feeling their anger grow, knowing I can't hold out forever. "Okay, you can have some sugarless gum," I say at last, feeling power seep out of me.

And then I feel desperate shame. I don't want the checker, or the other people in the store, or people I know, to find out I'm buying gum for my children, spoiling them, teaching them greed and lust. Letting people see you spend money is almost as bad as letting people see you have sex.

The summer our children were eight and six, my husband and I took them often to the Louisiana World's Fair; what they liked best was to go to the arcade and play Skeeball. These were family outings. It was not an option for me, then, to say to my husband: "You take them; I'd rather drink muddy water than spend another minute in that arcade."

So I stood in the dim aisle between the video games while bells rang and people thumped joy sticks and punched buttons and stared into the flat, abstract scenes on the screens. I felt like I was in hell. Our children asked for more money and my husband gave it to them, dollar bills, five-dollar bills. They changed them into quarters and put the quarters in the slot and rolled the balls up the incline to try to get them into the circle that paid the most points. Tickets came out when they made points, and they saved them, and just before the fair closed we went to the arcade for one final Skeeball orgy and at last they had enough tickets to get the most expensive prizes, a great big plush toucan and a giant alligator with a man on its chest.

I used to play Skeeball at Capitola, a beach resort we went to for weekends sometimes when I was growing up. I remember playing, but I can't remember getting the money from my father. My parents must have gone to the bar next to the arcade while I played, and when I wanted more money I must have stood in the doorway and waited for them to notice me—a minor couldn't enter a bar in California. I do remember the bar, the sun streaming in from the balcony overlooking the river, the shiny round tables. He gave me the money, but I think he hated me for asking. I was using up all his money. I was draining him dry. If it weren't for me he'd be comfortable, he'd be safe, but I was such a burden: The cost of my clothes and my amusements was going to break him.

He never had enough; and all his life he lived in fear that what he did have would be taken from him.

And I had to pay for that.

CHASING THE GOBLINS AWAY

There was a time in my life, before I knew I had been abused, when I cooked a hot breakfast for my dogs every morning. I mixed whole wheat flour, soybean flour, brewer's yeast, garlic powder, bone meal, eggs, corn oil, cod liver oil, wheat germ oil, and fresh grated vegetables, spread the batter in a jelly-roll pan, and baked it in the oven. If the vegetable du jour was onion, the kitchen smelled like quiche; if it was daikon, it smelled like Limburger cheese.

When one of my sons had a friend spend the night, they would pass through the kitchen on the way to Saturday morning cartoons, and the friend would blink sleepily at the jelly-roll pan cooling on top of the stove and ask, "What's that? Brownies?"

"Brownies?" my son would say, hope struggling with disbelief in his face, and then he would realize the truth. "Oh, that's just my mom's dog food."

During the same period I kept track of every morsel of food that passed my lips. I had a chart on the inside of one of the kitchen cabinets where I would record each item, along with the time of day, how many calories it had, how many grams of protein, and how many grams of fat. I also had a chart for each month, where I recorded my dietary score for each day and the total for each week according to a point system I had devised.

I believed that if I could just stick to a healthy diet—there was a series of them over the years—I would stop being anxious and depressed, would enjoy my children, would stand up straight and walk with a spring in my step, would, in short, become a perfect human being.

All my life I've had these fantasies of perfection and control. One summer a few years before I started therapy, I decided that my dog—just one dog then—had fleas because she didn't get enough affection. (This was right after the fruitless search for an orthomolecular veterinarian, though a year later I did find a holistic animal doctor in Texas who was willing to talk to me on the phone for forty dollars.) I set aside ten minutes a day, after I had picked the kids up at swimming lessons and dropped them off at tennis camp, for petting the dog. I kept it up for a week or so, and then, overcome by a rare fit of good sense, I said to myself: "To hell with this—I'm taking a nap!"

Most of the time, however, I approached these projects with complete seriousness and dedication. The carrot juice episode, for instance. One of my books recommended fresh vegetable juice to stimulate a sluggish digestive system, and mine was certainly sluggish after an abrupt switch from Dr. Cooper's Fabulous Fructose Diet to the Pritikin Program. I bought a juice extractor and began buying carrots by the sack. I did feel a lot better, and I noticed I was screaming at my children less often, though perhaps this was wishful thinking. But I was also turning orange. "You're a funny color," my doctor said when I consulted him about the headaches I was now having all the time.

"Oh, that's just because I drink a lot of carrot juice," I said. "Nothing to worry about."

"Your liver enzymes are elevated," he said.

"Oh," I said.

I didn't want to believe that I had done this to myself, but I had to, because as soon as I stopped drinking carrot juice, my enzymes dropped to normal and my headaches went away.

For a few weeks I felt I had reached a dead end, nutritionally. But then I found macrobiotics. In spite of an initial inability to distinguish between yin and yang, I followed the diet enthusiastically, drawn to its fundamentalism and its promise that if I ate a balanced diet I would never be angry.

My diets and charts are my drug. When I feel a surge of energy for organizing—color-coding the linen closet shelves, arranging the spice jars in alphabetical order, weeding out the appliance warranties file—then I know there is something trying to get me, some painful dissonance waiting to surface. That's when I want something to fill time, something to block those feelings of helplessness, desolation, and rage.

When I find myself standing in front of the refrigerator gobbling pecans by the handful, or stealing the children's Halloween candy, or eating a banana and then an apple and then a grapefruit and then a pear and then some raisins and then a peanut butter and jelly sandwich and then a bag of chocolate chips, that is also a sign of pain waiting to get me. "Pain deferred is pain not felt," a college friend used to say, and eating is one way of deferring the pain, of stuffing the feelings back inside, just as I hold my hands over my mouth when I cry.

For most of my life, it's been either famine or feast. Either I'm perfect and hang up my clothes as I take them off, skirts on one side of the closet, tops on the other, each garment in a space reserved for its color group; or I'm a slattern who lets her clothes pile up on a chair for days and days, clean and dirty all jumbled together. Either whole grains, vegetables, and beans three times a day, or sweet grease from breakfast till bedtime. Either a color-coded system, or chaos. When I'm "in control," my stomach is drawn up in a hard little ball. When I'm "out of control," my stomach is stretched and painful, stuffed with food I've eaten in a vain attempt to fill myself up.

The joy of asceticism: work work work; save save save. Never let anybody, especially yourself, catch you having fun. I tell myself I'd rather be playing, but I lie. Something in me wants cold baths and vegetables, wants to engineer a new self, wants to get more and more perfect until I finally win the war against my body.

Finding out what happened to me as a child has taught me to recognize my compulsive behavior as a way to stay in control and stifle pain. Such behavior is a signal, and therefore a blessing. Why am I making this list? Why am I eating these Necco Wafers? Sometimes I can stop long enough to ask the question, sometimes I can even stop long enough to let myself feel the pain. For a little while.

Some compulsions, of course, are worth pursuing for their own intrinsic beauty. Inside another cabinet—not the one where I used to keep my diet charts—are taped two dozen cards with single words written on them in bold black marker: ANTIBIOTIC. SUIT. EARDROPS. DRYER. GOMASIO. I love to open the cabinet and see them there, so reassuringly black-and-white.

"What are *those?*" my kids' friends ask.

"My mom's reminders."

"Oh. Right."

"She takes them out and tapes them up on the refrigerator when she wants to remember something."

"Oh. Sure. Right."

DEATH

My father died on a June day in 1979 while my husband and I and our children were vacationing in Florida. William was three, and had been to the beach once before in his short life; Tom, at thirteen months, had never seen sand except at the playground. We got out of the car and went straight to the water, and our children pushed each other down and rolled in the sand, laughing and hugging each other. As we watched them, my husband and I laughed and hugged each other too.

In California, my parents and their guests—a young couple

about the same age as my husband and me—had finished lunch and were getting ready to walk to the pool in their apartment complex for a swim. My father said he had a touch of indigestion, and told them to go on without him. Soon, however, he recognized the pain of his second coronary. He was sixty-seven; the first had struck him when he was forty-eight. He called the lifeguard to page my mother. Minutes later the paramedics arrived to take him to the hospital, the same hospital where he had performed surgery almost every day for almost thirty years.

In a description of his earlier attack, he had written about his feelings after the analgesic took effect: "Where the pain had been was an ache not unlike a deep sadness. It crossed my mind that the poetic 'death from a broken heart' was unquestionably a myocardial infarct related to grief."

Now he lay in Intensive Care, groggy from morphine but still conscious. "I'm going to make it," he told my mother.

In Florida, we got back from the beach to find a note from the office on our cottage door. I called my mother, and then I took William for a walk and told him that Grandpa was very sick and might die, and we were going to leave the next morning and go to California.

We put the children to bed. A friend's nephew came to stay in our cottage while we went for a walk on the beach, but I didn't want to be separated from my children even though they were asleep; and the noise of the waves seemed too loud.

My husband and I went back to the cottage and I thought about my father: about making rounds with him on Sundays, and the pancake breakfasts he used to fix for me afterwards; about riding bikes to Coyote Point and riding on his shoulders to get an ice-cream cone. I tried to use these memories to make myself cry. But I could not.

I believed it was my fault that our relationship had deteriorated after what I remembered as a warm, close childhood. At the time he died we were, as I saw it, in neutral, spinning our wheels. We spoke only of factual matters, never of how we felt, and our conversations were lifeless except when he had something to teach that I wanted to learn. My feelings were not engaged. Even if I had known how to take off my mask, I did not want to do that. The very thought of it frightened me, though I did not know why.

Always, as an adult, I felt I had to defend myself against him, to build a wall around myself. I saw myself, and the boundaries between me and him, as fragile. Whenever I felt myself letting go, I got scared and pulled back. And now I was unable to grieve for him.

In the cottage I found a Gideon Bible and read some psalms. We went to bed. I read a junk novel, dozed, and startled awake. It seemed very important to stay awake: Something awful would happen if I went to sleep.

The cottages had no telephones. If my mother called in the night she would have to call the office and ask the manager to come and get me. I knew that a knock on the door would mean my father was dead.

In the middle of the night, while I was dozing, the knock came. I went with the manager to the office and picked up the phone. "Mommy?" I said. She said, "He didn't make it."

We drove home, and all four of us flew to California. The morning after we arrived, my father's obituaries began appearing in the papers:

Dr. Clinton V. Ervin, Jr., 67, chief of staff at Crystal Springs Rehabilitation Center in San Mateo and a physician-surgeon for 40 years on the Peninsula, died Sunday night of a heart attack at Mills Memorial Hospital. During his career he held such positions as chief of surgical services at Southern Pacific Hospital, San Francisco; chief of staff [and chief of surgery] at Mills; chief of surgery at Peninsula Hospital, Burlingame; surgical staff member of

Chope Community Hospital; and assistant clinical professor of surgery on the faculty of the University of California Medical School in San Francisco. He was a reserve medical officer at Letterman General Hospital in the Presidio for four years during World War II, later went to Okinawa and rose to the rank of lieutenant colonel. . . . His many interests included alcohol rehabilitation. "I am interested in people and the process of making them well," he once summed up his far-ranging activities. Dr. Ervin was president of the San Mateo County Medical Society for three years, ending in 1975. . . . Dr. Ervin was a pioneer in the understanding of emotional problems connected with breast cancer. . . . He helped to found the Union of American Physicians and Dentists in the early 1970s in an effort to resist government restrictions that he felt interfered with patient care. In 1974, he retired from private practice and became staff physician for San Mateo County Crystal Springs Rehabilitation Center, a position he held until his death. . . .

My father's memorial service was to be held at St. Matthew's Episcopal Church, next door to Mills Hospital, where he worked and died. Although my parents attended church only for weddings, funerals, and the baptisms of their grandchildren, many of my father's colleagues were church members. The interim rector, who was new in town, opposed my suggestion that the congregation sing hymns at the service. Since my father had not been a member of the church, he said, the congregation would be small, and the hymns would seem weak and ineffectual. The church is going to be full, I wanted to say, but I lacked the energy.

After we talked with the priest, my mother and I went to a memorial service for my father at Crystal Springs Rehabilitation Center, where he worked after he retired from the practice of surgery. The dining room was full. There were nurses and staff members and patients, many of them in wheelchairs. I was told that the patients had organized the service. There were prayers and eulogies and songs. When we sang "Swing low, sweet chariot," I cried, but not enough to satisfy my desire for tears. When we sang "He's got the whole world in His hands," the leader added a verse: "He's got Dr. Ervin in His hands, He's got Dr. Ervin in His hands, He's got Dr. Ervin in His hands, He's got the whole world in His hands."

The next day the church was full, packed with colleagues and patients and friends and neighbors. Later my mother told me that when my father was dying, only one of his fellow physicians came to sit with her in the Intensive Care waiting room; and when he died, his doctor, a friend of many years, called her on the waiting room telephone to tell her he was gone. But on this day everyone had gathered: It might have been Easter. I deeply regretted the unsung hymns. I thought if only I could have sung "The strife is o'er, the battle done," or "Time, like an ever-rolling stream, bears all his sons away," I might have been able to cry.

An old friend of my parents, Gerald Egelston, sent a eulogy from New York which a friend of my father's read to the congregation:

For those who knew him as their doctor, he was first a gentle man, who inspired confidence with his first interview, and who elicited trust from his first touch on the examining table. He was a doctor who always laid on his hands for the patient, and they were touched physically, spiritually, and intellectually. Apprehension about an operation was usually lost to the comfort and confidence of knowing that this gentle, concerned man was to care for one. . . . Conversation with him was a delight. He was a man of catholic tastes, and his scientific mind retained everything he ever read, so conversation could move from social problems, to wines, to music, to fishing; from the antiquity of the redwoods to the muscular development of go-go dancers. All books were grist for his intellectual mill. He enjoyed argument and would take any side for the sake of lively discussion. . . . [He was] a man of great depths, depths best demonstrated by his capacity for caring and loving, and those many who loved and admired Clint as patient, colleague, friend, and family felt this gentle strength that warmed one.

After the service my mother and I stood in the back of the church while people filed by and hugged us and kissed us and talked of how much my father had meant to them. Then we went back to her apartment and ate the food her friends had brought. People stayed for a long time.

The next morning my mother and I got up at dawn and the hospital chaplain, who was also a pilot, came to drive us to a small airport on the coast. We brought my father's ashes in a container the size of a box of crackers. The chaplain checked out a small airplane and we took off into the brilliant blue sky. He fixed the automatic pilot so we would circle over the ocean. He asked us if we would like to read something from the Bible. My mother read the Twenty-third Psalm, and I read the Forty-sixth: "God is our refuge and strength, a very present help in trouble. Therefore we will not fear though the earth should change, though the mountains shake in the heart of the sea; though its waters roar and foam, though the mountains tremble with its tumult. There is a river whose streams make glad the city of God, the holy habitation of the Most High. God is in the midst of her, she shall not be moved; God will help her right early . . ."

The chaplain took out his pocketknife and slit open the wrapping on the box. He opened the window of the plane. He lifted the lid of the box. Inside were white shards of bone, like the white rocks people put in their flower beds. He held the box out the window and turned it over, and the pieces of bone flew out behind the plane and whirled down until they disappeared in the brightness of the sun on the water.

At my mother's apartment, condolence letters were arriving. The letters mentioned his kindness, his wit, his learning, his compassion. The word used most frequently was "gentle." Many commented on my parents' love for each other: how blessed they were to have each other's love, how happy my mother had made my father, how unusual it was to see a really caring relationship like theirs. My mother would have beautiful memories of my father, the letters said. Nothing would ever take those memories away from her.

CONDOLENCES

Every time I went to his office I felt at home with him, I never felt that way in other doctor offices. . . . He always made me feel good on my way out and carry good memories about him all the time. I will <u>never, never</u> forget Dr. Ervin as long as I live.

Clint gave me my first sense that I could become a competent person, that I could accomplish something with my life. He wrote my first recommendation to college, gave me a copy, and with it a subtle confidence in my own abilities. Clint always seemed to respect what I had to say, even though much of it seems sophomoric in retrospect. At a time when I was confused and unsure, he gave me a sense of my own worth. He not only had the ability to touch what was warm and positive in me and in others, but he also was able with his gentle humor to put life's upsets into proper perspective. Once, after a particularly hysterical evening with Dad, Clint came over, talked to me, held my hand until the tears and gasps left. While I don't recall what he said to me, I do remember that by the time he left I was smiling.

From the daughter of my father's friend

You and Dr. Ervin have meant so much to me. I have just loved you both. I want you to know how much I will miss Dr. Ervin. It seems that the whole world should stop.

From my best friend in high school

He was one of the truly great friends and companions of my life. He gave me my first surgery to do when I came to San Mateo and he continued for twenty-seven years to enrich my life with his kindness, wisdom, example, leadership, inspiration, under-standing, consolation, encouragement . . . When you thought you knew him, he'd pop up with a new expression or dimension to confound, amuse, and to thrill you. Clint's quiet modesty provided a striking contrast with the magnitude of the man who possessed it.

I always felt that he was one of my great mentors and shall always feel that he contributed as much or more to my development as anyone with whom I trained. . . . Our lives have all been enriched by knowing him.

From a professor at Harvard Medical School

He was truly a gentleman and a real libertarian. His surgical acumen and skill speak for themselves. One of the proud recollections of my early years is when Clint and I passed a motion in the Medical Society condemning the state "loyalty oath"—later declared unconstitutional. It was fun to be associated with someone whose sense of freedom and dignity was reflected from within and made all about him more worthwhile.

Clint had an exceptional mind. He was superb at identifying fundamental problems and explaining them. I felt that I could always get a clear and constructive view from him on surgical problems. He was so good at recognizing personality problems.

He impressed me most as a very warm and kind individual, with a marvelous sense of humor, who enjoyed his life and the lives of those around him. Something unique about him was the ease with which he could make others feel so comfortable. Even now I can fondly look back to that time in my life and feel as if I was "family." Since then I've met and known many other men and many who I've liked but only a few that I can say I've really admired—yet that's the way I feel about Clint.

From my first boyfriend

Clint was that rare combination—a thinker and a doer. But more than that he cared and he really tried to make the world a more decent place. Every meeting with Clint was a delight—because he was nice and smart and funny—and good to be around.

As a new grad in 1952, I worked for Dr. Ervin at the Clinic. He was kind, helpful, and patient. His superior surgical skills were well known to all, but, I think, equally important—he was a teacher of trust, gentleness, and <u>real</u> caring. Watching him deal with patients' illnesses and problems with such sensitivity was an invaluable lesson to me, as a nurse.

Clint was one of my oldest, wisest, most reliable friends. He was also a dear man in the sense that he was gentle, compassionate, temperate in judgment, lovable and, as a doctor, unremitting in his devotion to patients, wise in diagnosis, skillful in execution. He lifted my gangrenous appendix and I lost only thirty-six hours from the office. For many things I am thankful . . . that his passing was blessedly short, that he had a full life, weathering its storms and surviving with dignity and with the immense respect of all his peers. God blessed Clint in these ways.

"TRUTH IS A
RELATIVE
MATTER"

In the fall of my senior year in college, after my sister had left her husband for Max, I became involved in a romantic triangle and felt unable to commit myself to either boyfriend. Upset and miserable, I called my parents seeking a way out of the situation. My father wrote this letter in response to my call, but never mailed it; I found it in the box of letters sent to me by my mother twenty-five years later.

Your phone call raised more questions than I can possibly answer, much as I would like to do so.

First of all we thank you for calling us when you felt in need. May you always do so. My comments on honesty with respect to Pat unquestionably disturbed you & probably should never have been made, since her reasons are to her good ones. Truth is an elusive concept & a highly subjective one. We are forever separated from reality by the inadequacy of our senses & we color our observations by our moods & emotions of the moment. Our intellectual processing of the data observed is often faulty & our memories of the whole may be grossly inaccurate. It all adds up, to me at least, to the concept that truth is a relative matter, being never the same from two separate points in either time or space.

How difficult it is to be truthful when truth is not clear cut & stable. We are taught to expect white & black in life when all the world is in color & even shades of gray have pastel tinges.

So telling the truth is difficult, technically. Why try at all? That it is "expected of us" by our hypocritical culture is hardly an adequate reason. The two reasons I can see are to preserve the faith which someone I love has in me or for vital self-protection or preservation. It immediately follows that faith [crossed out] the best interests [crossed out] may not always be best served by the truth, certainly not if it is unsolicited. The truth can be very cruel & not everyone who asks it wants it. Often evasion by misdirection, by tone of voice or change of subject (the old "switcheroo"), a question instead of an answer, partial or total omission, a difference in emphasis, may serve. The nearer one stays to the facts the easier to escape consequences if caught. One should always keep this possibility in mind & be prepared with something like "You misunderstood" or "I was mistaken" or "I really didn't mean what I said." If faced with the necessity for an out-and-out falsehood make it plausible, simple, & as brief as possible. Then change the subject. If caught be prepared to say "I only did it for your sake." The really skillful liar will say: "You made me do it. It's all your fault." But making this convincing requires more practice than I hope you will acquire.

And now what about the occasions when you are on the receiving end? A few simple test questions will usually establish the evasion, and it is usually better to let the matter lie, since to pursue it produces more in grief than in information.

What about the faith one person has in another? It is the projection of his own security, and jealousy is a manifestation of its lack. True, one may be realistically insecure, as when a love is not reciprocated or is lost, but jealousy is more often the reflection of a deeper insecurity often completely unrelated to the fancied threat.

The question "Have you been unfaithful to me?" should never be asked. Faith and truth are equated, rightly or wrongly, and the doubts inherent in asking this question can only be intensified by distrust in its answer. Almost any social relationship between a man & a woman has sexual overtones & the limits are prescribed by the culture. There is much hypocrisy in this area, & society seems quite satisfied with discretion. For yourself, set your own limits, & not too rigidly, & don't feel guilty if or when they differ from limits set by others. And do not fall into the trap of requiring another to conform to your own limits. Setting limits for another is an exercise in self-deception—he will resent your act in setting them even if they coincide with his own, & he may rebel for no other reason.

GOD

One evening I went straight from my incest survivors' therapy group to a Great Books discussion of Machiavelli. The evening seemed all of a piece. In group we talked about wanting to be taken care of by trustworthy parents—wanting what we couldn't have. At Great Books we talked about Machiavelli's manual on "how to be a fine liar and hypocrite," his advice to the prince to "appear, when seen and heard, to be all compassion, all faithfulness, all integrity, all kindness." That was my father, all compassion and integrity to his friends, colleagues, and patients. Yet he was also a child molester. If the concept of vice has any meaning, he was truly vicious.

If he were alive to defend himself, that would be his defense: The concept of vice has no meaning. Everything is relative. There is no standard of virtue that is not determined by culture and self-interest; there is no firm ground to stand on; there is no such thing as "reality."

When I was three I went to Sunday school in a restaurant. The church had grown too fast to hold all the children, so the congregation rented or borrowed the restaurant to hold the overflow. I was there because I had asked to go—my friends at nursery school went to church, and I wanted to go, too, so my mother took me.

The neighborhood was cold and foggy, never warmed, in my memory, by a single ray of sunlight. Yet in my memory the restaurant is warm, heated by sun that streams through Venetian blinds and makes stripes on the tabletops. Outside, as we walk down a sloping street and across a busy thoroughfare back to our apartment, clouds blow across the sun, and by the time we get home all is gray and foggy once more.

That was church for me as I was growing up: a warm refuge, a sunny place where my father did not go. I felt funny in church, like an outsider, never sure what the rules were or what was expected of me. But I liked singing the hymns, and I liked the warm, plain church with its soft carpet underfoot and its polished brown wood behind the altar.

I did not look for God in church. People went there to talk about Him, not to meet Him. My parents did not talk about Him, except when I asked direct questions. I remember sitting on my father's lap while he told me that different people had different ideas about God—all, he gave me to understand, equally valid, or equally illusory.

In this area he was not a hypocrite. He rejected the Southern Baptist dogmas of his childhood, which were repressive and judgmental, and in their place he offered reason and speculation.

Sometimes I would say prayers—"Now I lay me down to sleep" or the Lord's Prayer—because I understood from my friends that one was supposed to. But I never imagined that God was actually listening.

One night when I was nine or ten I lay in my bed upstairs listening to an argument begin down in the living room. "What's the matter, honey?" my father said softly. "You know," my mother answered coldly. At first I tried to hear what they were saying, in case I might be affected by it, but as they got angrier, I tried not to hear. But I couldn't shut out the words. "Do you want a divorce?" I heard my father murmur.

My mother spit out her answer: "Yes!"

"When?"

"Tomorrow!"

I wasn't old enough to know that "tomorrow" meant she didn't mean it. I put my pillow over my head and cried until I began to feel desperate about the crying itself: I would be overwhelmed by it, and they would hear me and come into my room, and I couldn't bear it if they did.

"Please, God," I prayed over and over, "make them stop." But they did not stop. Finally, I prayed, "Please, God, make me stop crying." I felt something like a loving hand laid on my chest, firmly but not heavily. My breathing slowed, my tears stopped, and sleep shut out the rest of the quarrel.

By the time I was in high school, I had acquired these beliefs about religion: Some people worship the sun, and some people worship trees, and some people worship hallucinations. Most people are either Christians or Jews. Christians are sober, straitlaced people who want you to live just the way they do, and Jews are interesting, glamorous people who have outgrown

God. There are two kinds of Christians, with two kinds of God: Catholics worship a crucifix that hangs on the wall behind the altar, and Protestants worship a giant who sits on a throne above the sky. The God of the Catholics will send you to hell if you miss Mass, and the God of the Protestants will send you to hell if you take a drink.

Nevertheless, as soon as I could drive, I drove myself to church. One Sunday morning after my parents had been up late drinking the night before, my mother heard me moving around in the living room; the walls were thin, and I was making noise to annoy them. "Where are you going?" she called out, her voice thin and querulous.

"To church," I said.

"Oh, God!" she moaned.

I went to the Episcopal church because I loved singing the canticles at Morning Prayer: "O be joyful in the Lord, all ye lands," and "Blessed art thou, O Lord God of our fathers: praised and exalted above all forever." The ancient words, the simple, powerful music, the sound of my voice blending with all the others: I loved it so much that suddenly I found I believed every word of the Apostles' Creed. But it didn't stick, especially after college courses in philosophy, Western Civilization, and the history of science. There were too many creeds; how could any of them be valid? I decided to be an atheist—there was more certainty to it, if less comfort.

A few months after I graduated from college, I stood in the file room next to my office at the *Boston Globe* while people rushed back and forth in the hall with the latest bulletins from the Associated Press, or sat at their desks and cried: President Kennedy had just been shot in Dallas.

I was still an atheist, though reading Milton in college had humbled me a bit. "Better to rule in hell than serve in heaven," Milton had his devil say. Like generations of students, I had tried to prove the devil was the real hero of *Paradise Lost,* but I had failed.

Now, standing in the file room, I said to myself: "I refuse to live in a world where what's happening right now has no meaning." I decided to believe in God and then I decided to go to church and be instructed and baptized. I asked the teacher who had read Milton with me to be my godfather.

After I got religion, my father delighted in needling me. One day during a visit home we were walking together down a hot, dusty country road. "Tell me," he said, and I could hear the chortle in his voice as he got ready to skewer me with his logic, "can God make a rock so big He can't lift it?"

"I don't know," I snapped back. "But He can make a man He can't save."

He was silent, for once, and so was I. I was ashamed of my arrogance, and sorry I had refused to engage with my father in the debate he so enjoyed. I called this impulse to protect myself "sin."

Now I know it was legitimate to protect myself from my father. And yet I also know that alienation—from God, from other people, from oneself—is sin. Because of what my father did to me, I have been alienated from my husband and from my children. All my adult life I have struggled with my defenses: my fear of trusting others, my habit of clicking off or drifting away instead of being really present in the moment, my sense of fragile boundaries needing constant maintenance. For me these are spiritual problems as well as psychological ones, problems which, although I did not make them, are mine to struggle with and overcome. I refuse to live in a world where people aren't responsible for what they do. My father was responsible for what he did, and I am responsible for what I do.

When God began to heal me by revealing my history, He gave me the strength to bear the pain of that revelation. But I had to be willing to bear it. And then I had to bear it. And then I had to endure the terror of acting like a changed person before I felt like one.

There are certain hymns I can't sing without crying. The ones about suffering: "O Love that wilt not let me go,/I rest my weary soul in thee," written by a blind priest; and "They cast their nets in Gallilee," about the martyrdom of the apostles, which ends, "The peace of God it is no peace,/But strife closed in the sod./Yet, brothers, pray for but one thing—/The marvelous peace of God." And the ones about the joy that can still be found in a world full of suffering: "This is the hour of banquet and of song," which we sing at the Eucharist; and the Easter hymn, "Come ye faithful, raise the strain/Of triumphant gladness;/God hath brought his Israel/Into joy from sadness," which we sang at a beloved friend's funeral, belting it out as a challenge to our grief.

Even writing the words brings tears: for all the innocents who suffer as I did, for the anguish of all who, like me, have been afraid to be close, afraid to trust anyone; for the awful, awful things that people do to one another, and for the darkness of denial, when people won't bear the pain of looking at what was done, won't believe that forgiveness and healing—redemption—are a real possibility.

Must I forgive my father? If to forgive means to be healed, to move beyond the place where he still has the power to hurt me, I want to do that. But I don't want to give away my anger at what he did, to say it doesn't matter, or that he was only acting out his own history. I need my anger to fuel my own healing, and he deserves it. Let God love him; I don't want to get that close.

Maybe, though, I can learn to live with the paradox that inheres in the world: He was responsible for what he did, but he was also innocent once, and a victim. And no matter how corrupt he became, many people received compassion and, literally, new life from him.

I still have problems with the concept of God the father. But as I remember my husband walking the floor with our colicky baby held against his chest, murmuring softly, "It's not easy to be a baby," I begin to understand. As for God the mother, is it presumptuous to imagine that I'm learning to know Her as I experience my love for our sons? A mother can't make the world a safe place for her children. But she can be with them when they hurt.

Some people find themselves unable to believe in a God who lets the innocent suffer; but for me the suffering of the innocent is a consequence of the freedom to choose, of the gift of responsibility. God wants us to love one another as She loves us, but She doesn't make us do it. We are free to choose darkness instead of light.

Sometimes it is hard to choose the light. Sometimes even now when I try to pray, I hear my father's voice. "Don't be fooled," he whispers. "You will never find God. You will never find your true self. There is no God. You have no true self."

The world is a terrible place, a place where parents rape their children. But I can still feel God's hand on my chest, so different from the hand of my father. I refuse to live in my father's world, a world barren of all motives but the hunger for sensation and the lust for power. A few years before he died, he wrote this poem:

> In the sunlight
> the pool of life is bright
>   silver
> and all that lies beneath
>   the surface
> is hidden.

But when the sky
is darkened by a cloud
the reflection fades and
one can see with dreadful
  clarity
the fears and depths below.

can it be
that all the beauty in life
is but a reflection
  on the surface

"Can it be that all the beauty in life is but a reflection on the surface?" My answer is no. No, no, no.

TERROR, RAGE,
AND GRIEF

In the dream, my husband and I have moved into a house that needs a lot of work. Everything we own is jumbled together, our furniture crowded into the rooms any which way, mess and disorder everywhere. The front door has been hacked with an ax, and a big square piece of it, including the lock, has been sawed out. The door is patched with warped, weathered pieces of thin plywood; it cannot be locked. Workmen are in and out at all hours; I wake up and hear them talking in the next room, and sometimes they come right into the bedroom.

Snakes are hiding in the debris, thick as my arm, with

black and gray diamond-patterned bodies and triangular heads. They poke their heads out and stare at me, and I scream and try to run away and stumble over the furniture.

One night I'm home alone, feeling vulnerable in the house —anyone could come in through the damaged front door. My husband comes home and gets in bed with me, but when I wake up, scared, he is gone. I call and call but he doesn't come. A snake flicks its tongue in and out as it stares at me in a matter-of-fact way, knowing it has all the power. I know I am dreaming, and I think: This is my sister's snake phobia.

Then I am in a hotel, riding up in an elevator. I go into a room and see a woman who in waking life was a dear friend until her death a few years ago. Like my father, she was tall, heavy, and strong, dark-haired, with a southern accent. In the dream she holds a young girl on her lap, a girl who in waking life is the sister of a close friend. She is thin, with breasts just budding. The woman is fully clothed; the girl is naked.

The girl jumps up from the woman's lap and says, "Let's go swimming!" She is scowling, belligerent. The woman starts talking, fast, spinning an irrelevant yarn. I realize they are trying to distract me. I think: I need to tell someone that this girl is being molested.

The woman grabs me and holds me on her lap. I struggle but I can't get away. She has a penis; I can feel it hard against my buttocks. She moves my body against hers, and I know she is trying to have an orgasm.

Then I am back in the jumbled bedroom. A snake pokes its head out and looks at me, and I scream and scream, but nobody hears me.

Terror. In another dream I stand among bald people whose heads tip up like hinged lids, and a wailing sound fills the air

148

and I think I'll drown in it. The terror is about being unprotected, vulnerable to the full intensity of other people's emotions. There are no boundaries; their feelings overwhelm them and flow out and overwhelm me.

Years ago I smoked some marijuana, and felt waves of intense pleasure all over my body—followed by waves of terror. It was killing me. The pleasure was killing me; the terror was killing me. I was dying, going down into hell, where worms would eat my body and I would know it was happening but I couldn't make it stop.

Bliss, terror, bliss, terror, wave after wave, until I turned inside out and vomited. That was the horror I was trying to escape from when I dissociated during lovemaking: a time bomb set by my father.

In therapy I screamed over and over: "I don't want to feel this way, *I don't want to feel this way,* I DON'T WANT TO FEEL THIS WAY!"

Kris held me close, the way I wanted my mommy to hold me, and I heard her soft voice saying, "These are the feelings. This is why sex is not for children."

"Nobody would help me," I said. "I couldn't call for help. Nobody would come to help me." My voice sounded like a child's. "And he wouldn't stop. He wouldn't stop!"

"He wouldn't leave you alone," she said, stroking my hair. We sat quietly for a moment. "You couldn't tell anybody then," she said, "but now you can. You never, never have to be alone with this again."

Rage. Getting in touch with your anger is supposed to be a good thing to do if you were sexually abused as a child.

But it's not easy.

A friend tried hitting her bed with a tennis racket. She

imagined she was smashing her father's penis to a pulp—"And while I was hitting him I told him how I felt about what he did to me."

"What did you say?" I asked.

"I said, 'What you did was really inappropriate.' "

For a long time I couldn't even say that much.

I knew I had to do something about putting that anger where it belonged so I could stop lashing out at my children and my husband. But I felt stupid. I was afraid of looking small and ineffectual, absurd, like Rumpelstiltskin stomping a hole in the floor and getting his foot stuck. My father would be there, smiling the way he used to smile when I bellowed at him for pulling the dog's ears.

I did get out my tennis racket, but as soon as I hit the bed I started to cry. I was not entitled to my anger. Nobody would listen—I was all alone with it just as I had always been.

I dropped the racket and lay down on the floor, intending to pound it with my fists. But I couldn't. I held my arms close to my sides, my elbows bent and my fists pinned under me. I was able to kick the floor with my feet and stretch my mouth open as wide as it would go and scream—but I tightened my throat to muffle the scream, and pressed my face into the rug.

I addressed my father: "You didn't respect my boundaries." I wanted something stronger. "I hate you!" I screamed. "I hate you! I hate you! I hate you!" But the feelings wouldn't come. I just felt stupid.

I pressed my face into the floor so the neighbors wouldn't hear me and call the police, but at the same time I wanted to say: Call the police! I want the police to come and lock you up and never let you out, never never never never!

Then the words did flow, and they were very simple words: "Leave me alone, leave me alone, leave me alone! Don't touch me, don't touch me! Go away, go away, GO AWAY! DON'T TOUCH ME! LEAVE ME ALONE!''

I wanted a witness to my anger, but I was afraid. I told Kris: "There's a wall between me and my anger." I could see the wall. It was made of old brick, and at the bottom there was no grass, just dry dust and patches of weeds. It was tall, taller than my head, and there were no handholds or footholds. I couldn't climb it. I imagined myself beating on it, but my fists made no sound, and the rough surface scraped the skin off my knuckles and made them bleed.

Kris said, "We're going to take out one brick, just one, down at the bottom, and peek through. The rest of the wall will still be intact."

I peeked through the hole, and saw a foot, big and hairy, with claws—the foot of a monster from Maurice Sendak's *Where the Wild Things Are*. The monster was my anger. The monster was my father.

I felt defeated. I wanted a real monster, not a cute one. How ludicrous to get angry at a cute monster. Sendak's monsters wanted to play all night. Was my father only playing? "I only wanted to make you feel good," he would say, if he were alive to say it. "You liked it—you know you did. I wouldn't hurt you for anything in the world."

In a dream I am standing in a bare room with my mother and father and a group of strangers. My father wears a blue polyester Mexican wedding shirt. He is plump and stooped over, smiling like a dog confronted with its mess. "I'm sorry," he whines. "I never wanted to hurt you." He tries to put his arm around me.

I step back. "Don't touch me," I warn him. My voice is loud but controlled. "You can never touch me again," I say, speaking slowly as one does to a child who habitually misbehaves. "I can never be alone with you again, and you can never touch me again."

He smiles, hangs his head, and tries again to put his arm around me.

"You. Can. Never. Touch. Me. Again," I repeat.

Once again he smiles foolishly and tries to put his arm around me. But then he lets it drop and shakes his head: I'm being harsh and unreasonable, but he'll humor me.

I want a huge, powerful monster, smelly and hairy and bellowing, whose footfalls make the earth shake. And indeed that is just how he was when I was a child. I want him to stay that way, to hold still for my anger. And I want Kris to get a bulldozer and knock down that wall in an explosion of noise and dust so I can get at him.

But I know I have to take it down myself.

I got out a picture of me in my Brownie uniform. My father didn't take it, as he did most of our family photographs; one of the mothers had come and taken pictures of the whole troop. My bangs are pushed back under my Brownie headband, and I'm smiling into the camera. I still have all my baby teeth. I'm six years old. At night my father is coming to my room and putting his fingers between my legs, and he won't stop.

I put my picture in a frame on my desk. So I could see how cute I was, and how young, and how deserving of protection, when he was doing that to me. But the rage won't come. Not yet.

But I have been very, very angry with my mother. Where was she when my father was doing those things to me? Why didn't she protect me? Why didn't she know it was happening?

Now I can feel my anger slipping away, and I don't want to let it go. Anger keeps my mother close to me. When I stop being mad at her she'll be gone, sliding off the planet away from me into outer space. As long as I am angry, I am hoping that someday, if I keep trying to make her listen, she will want to know what happened to me. Yet I also want a cleaner rage, one that does not hope, or stop to ask "Did I go too far?" A rage that does not seek a response from another, but only exists: something of my own.

Grief. That my Daddy, who bought me ice-cream cones and carried me on his shoulders, did those things to me. I want to feel that grief, but it eludes me; just as I wanted to grieve for my father when he died, but could not. Where is the Daddy I wished for, the Daddy I never had and never will have? What would it be like to have a Daddy who could be trusted, a Daddy who found me delightful just because I existed? In my father's eyes I had no reality apart from him: Everything I did, everything I was, was a reflection of him.

I won't let myself think about the Daddy I didn't have. It hurts too much. It doesn't feel safe: wanting and wanting and not getting what I want. Nor am I ready to grieve for my mother. I grieve not yet for my loss but for hers, the loss of her daughters' childhood, the closeness she might have had with us but did not.

I wake up at night with a dry mouth, breathing fast and heavy, muttering, "Oh, no! Oh, no!" It's about my father, but it's about her, too: Something has happened or is going to happen and my mother is not there. I am alone, and she's not coming. She's gone. She was always gone.

At a gathering of artists, writers, and musicians who had been abused as children, a woman showed her etchings. She passed them around the circle as if they were snapshots from her vacation: "Here I am tied up in the basement; there's the washing machine, and there's my father's shadow. This is me and my brother. He used to make us take off our clothes and lie down and pretend . . . This is me working as a stripper. I call it 'Self Worth.' This is me cutting my wrists."

The subject was so ugly but the work was so beautiful. The curving line of the children's naked bodies pressed together, echoed by the belt raised to strike . . . I wanted to stay with it, to affirm the way this woman had transformed what was done to her.

Another woman, who had also been tied up and tortured as a child, said, "I have trouble believing people actually do things like this. It helps me to see your pictures, to know it really happened."

I believe with all my heart that people should tell what was done to them, tell as clearly and powerfully as they can. Yet when I looked at the pictures, I went someplace and didn't even know I had gone. It was eight hours before I started to cry, before I knew that I had protected myself the way I always protect myself, by withdrawing into a spare, clean, empty place in a corner of my mind.

So how can I expect to get my mother's attention with my story? The more powerfully I tell it, the farther away she will go.

In the picture the boy and girl, pressed together under their father's blows, hold their arms close to their sides, their elbows bent and their fists pinned under them. They stretch their mouths open to scream, but because it is a picture, their screams have no sound. What are they screaming?

This is what I heard when I looked at the picture: I want my mommy! I want my mommy! I want my mommy!

BODYWORK

I couldn't go to the bathroom so I had to go to the doctor.

My colon was full of shit and my head was full of dialogues. Even though this doctor was a woman, my anxiety would not go away. She would say: *You're malingering.* Or, *You have cancer.* Or both.

She would look deep into the dark, secret places inside me, would see the impacted experiences I ate and never digested, lodged in the twists and turns of the colon, in little alcoves and niches, sticking to the walls like barnacles and growing, turning from a dirty secret unexpelled stool into a dirty secret cancer. I was afraid she might see how dirty I was, might say: "What have you been doing, you dirty girl?"

Going to the doctor was worse when I went to a man. He would be mad at me for wasting his time, would go home and tell his wife I'm a crock or some stupid woman with tired housewife's syndrome. But I went anyway. If I didn't, maybe it really was cancer, growing deep inside, eating me up silently, with only the smallest, most ambiguous signs to warn me.

When I was in college I went to a gynecologist colleague of my father's for a routine checkup, a look at some small symptoms of some kind, fatigue maybe. After he examined me and told me I was fine, I said in a small voice, "You mean I'm not going to die?" I was trying to make a joke, but I can still hear my voice, high and scared and begging to be reassured. The voice of one of those crocks who wasted my father's time.

I went to see the nice lady doctor, and she said my lab work looked fine, but I should get a sigmoidoscopy anyway, just in case. She explained how a long, flexible tube would be inserted in my rectum and moved high up into my colon, and the doctor would look through it as he worked it up inside me.

He would see all my secrets.

On the morning of the sigmoidoscopy, I saw my therapist. "I have to go get a tube stuck up me," I said at the end of the session, laughing to show I appreciated the irony of it. She did not laugh. "Where are your feelings?" she asked.

"Oh, right! Feelings! I should be having feelings about this, shouldn't I?" I was still smiling.

"Call me when you get home from the doctor," she said.

I drove to the gastroenterologist's office. He was a pleasant, self-effacing man who made sympathetic references to the anxiety he said everyone feels about what he was about to do. I made polite conversation with him, lay quietly while he moved his scope around the corners of my colon, listened impassively to his news that there was nothing unusual to be seen, and thanked him when I left. But as soon as I got inside my car and locked the door, I began to whimper.

I was a little wounded animal, gone to ground in my lair, shut into my car in the dark parking garage. I wrapped my arms around my body and hunched my shoulders and drew my knees up under the steering wheel. I keened, and I heard my cries, loud inside the closed-up car. I had no words, no thoughts. Someone bigger and stronger had done something to me, hurt me. I didn't know what. I didn't know who. I didn't know why.

I started going to exercise class because the other women in my writers' group went, and we couldn't find a time to meet, and Erie said, "Why don't you come to class and we'll meet afterwards at the coffee place down the street?" Grumbling a little, I went. I had never considered doing such a thing: It seemed so self-indulgent, so prodigal of time, to spend twenty minutes driving there and an hour and fifteen minutes doing it and twenty more minutes driving home, and the morning half gone and nothing to show for it.

I loved it from the first minute. I was dancing! As a child I wanted to take ballet, but my father wouldn't allow it. His judgment, relayed through my mother, was that they didn't know enough about ballet to choose a good teacher, and a bad one would put me on point too soon and ruin my legs.

As I think about it now, angry tears prickle against my eyelids. He acted like he knew everything about everything else, why not this? He was always doing research on things that interested him, why not this? They gave me swimming lessons, trampoline lessons, tennis lessons, horseback-riding lessons. But those were all things they wanted me to do. The one thing I wanted, they would not give me. I had nothing of my own; my father made sure of that. He wasted the time I could have spent dancing.

When I was eight or nine, I checked a ballet book out of the library and practiced the basic positions in the living room, using the back of the sofa as a barre. At college I joined the modern dance group and stayed in it for four years. But after graduation I stopped dancing, for the same reasons I resisted going to exercise class: It was self-indulgent, wasteful of time.

I hadn't realized how much I missed it. The rock music was mostly unfamiliar, but the beat was the beat of my adolescence. It sang to me of independence, of breaking away from my parents, of a time when I could dance with boys my own age. Could flirt, and be safe. Dancing to a record player in someone's backyard, to music with a raunchy beat but innocent words, was appropriate teenage behavior, just as if I really were an innocent young girl with choices about what to do with my body. Now, dancing in exercise class, I felt that my body had been given back to me.

Then one morning I woke up with a backache. *This is what you get,* said a voice in my head. *You should have known you'd never get away with it.* The voice said my body was too fragile; I'd pushed it too hard. It said my dancing days were over.

I remembered being a child in Mrs. Maxey's third-grade class. One day my back started to hurt and I went and stood beside her desk. There were several kids showing her their papers, and I stood there, waiting for her to see me. It hurt so bad and I couldn't speak. I stood there thinking: I can't talk.

She looked up and saw me. "Yes, Betsy?" I just stood there. "Betsy?" she said. I stood there, looking into her face the way my dog looks into my face sometimes, wanting her to understand that I couldn't speak and I needed her help. What kind of help I didn't know.

Then I was in the principal's office and Mrs. Maxey was calling my mother, and the pain was going away. I felt embarrassed and ashamed. It was stupid of me to bother everybody and make such a fuss, when it was nothing after all.

I suppose my father must have hurt my back, lying on top of me. He was so big, and I was so small. I can't remember—but my body remembers. When, as an adult, my back started to hurt, I felt ashamed. I went into my bedroom and closed the door and got down on my hands and knees and cried as waves of shame engulfed me. These were the tears and the feelings I had blocked as I stood by Mrs. Maxey's desk. If it had felt safe then to want anything, I would have wanted her to make my father stop doing that to me.

Now I didn't want to see the physical therapist. I was afraid she'd be mad at me for hurting my back, afraid she'd tell me I couldn't dance anymore, afraid she'd tell me the pain was all in my mind. I told myself I didn't have time to wait in her office; it would take too long; I would have to rearrange my schedule; I had too much to do.

But if I didn't go, I couldn't dance, so I went. One of my lumbar vertebrae was rotated. The physical therapist pushed and pulled on my back, applied heat and ice, gave me exercises to do, and told me to go back to class as soon as the pain was gone.

My body. Sometimes the sight of it in the mirror is too much for me. Then the choreography, complicated enough to demand my undivided attention, gives me a place in my mind to escape to; and the beat gives me a way to get back, back into my body.

Exercise class feels even better than those teenage backyard parties. I'm dancing with myself, in a place where it is safe to unfold my arms and legs and straighten up out of the defensive posture I assumed as a child. I was weak then, but now I am strong. I can lift my one-pound weights as many times as the music calls for, eight, sixteen, thirty-two. It hurts but it doesn't hurt so bad I have to stop. Those arms that stayed folded up against my body, those fists that could not punch, are free now.

One day I made up a chant to go with a routine that included a lot of punching and kicking. "MY body, MY body," I chanted to myself, and then, as I imagined myself kicking my father's face, "You're DEAD, you're DEAD!" Driving home in the car afterwards, I thought: You bastard. You asshole. You took away the closeness my children offered me when they were small. I couldn't receive it because of what you did to me, and now I can never get back that time. You stole it from me, the way you stole my innocence.

As I drove past the canal—the same dirty drainage canal I swam in with my father in a dream—I pushed the words out and screamed them: "You bastard, YOU BASTARD!" until I wore them out and only pure sound would do: "Agggggghhhhh-hhhh!" I screamed so hard the light seemed to grow dim, and I realized how foolish it was to endanger myself. I pulled over to the side of the road and waited until my vision cleared, and drove home to my children.

The next time we did the routine I listened to the words of the song for the first time. It was a song by INXS ("in excess") called "The Devil Inside," which tells of a man "fed on nothing but full of pride." The chorus goes: "The Devil inside/The Devil inside/Every single one of us/The Devil inside."

My body. My arms won't straighten, my hips are so tight I can't sit up in a straddle position, but my body is sturdy and reliable. It does what I ask it to do, awkwardly at first, but with growing strength and agility. When I'm tired and out of breath, I say to myself: Trust the beat.

There I am in the mirror, in the same leotard and tights I wore to modern dance class in college: dancing. I think I look pretty good, all in black like a real dancer. But even if I didn't, it wouldn't matter. Heavy women, clumsy women, dance beside me. I imagine that their impassive faces conceal the same outrageous joy as mine.

GOING PUBLIC

I've been having a recurring fantasy that I'm the defendant in a criminal trial. The charge: blackening my father's name, breaking my mother's heart. I'm on the stand. I've told my story. The prosecutor gets up to cross-examine me. "Mrs. Petersen," he begins, "what is your occupation?"

"I'm . . . a writer," I falter, afraid of what's coming next.

He turns away from me, his back rigid with disapproval, and walks toward the jury. "Isn't it true, Mrs. Petersen," he says, pitching his words at the men and women in the jury box, "that you are a writer of"—he pauses dramatically, turns back to face me, and then throws the word in my face—"*fiction?*"

I gather my courage and smile slightly, Walter Mitty about to take charge in the operating room. I murmur, "All of my *fiction* is still unpublished, Mr. Prosecutor."

"Oh, really?" he retorts in a voice heavy with sarcasm, and then, softly, menacingly, he goes on. "Your father was a great humanitarian, was he not? Kind, gentle, compassionate?"

"Everyone said so," I reply.

"Then *this*, Mrs. Petersen, must be fiction"—he holds up a copy of my book—"or else the work of a madwoman. You must be crazy to say he'd do a thing like that."

"What he did to me was enough to make me crazy," I say, keeping my voice level. "But he didn't succeed. I survived. I functioned. I flourished."

"Then you must be an out-and-out liar," says the prosecutor. "Sexual abuse is a hot topic right now. Aren't you just climbing on the bandwagon to advance your career?"

"I didn't set out to write a book, Mr. Prosecutor. It began as a therapeutic exercise, an attempt to deal privately with my anguish. Though it's certainly true that other writers' books have helped me get the courage to tell my own story."

The prosecutor walks toward the stand until he is standing too close to me. "Very well. I'm willing to believe"—only for the sake of argument, his tone implies—"that you have not deliberately lied. But isn't it possible, just remotely possible, that you might be mistaken? How in the world can you expect us to believe that you *forgot* something of such importance?"

"It's a common phenomenon, Mr. Prosecutor. And amnesia is particularly likely to occur when the victim is abused before puberty." I take from my purse some sheets of paper stapled together, a copy of an article by cognitive psychologist John Bowlby. "Listen to this." I tilt my head back so I can read the small print through my bifocals. " 'The father behaves during the day as though the nightly episodes never occurred, and this total failure to acknowledge them is commonly maintained even long after the daughter has reached adolescence. . . . [There is a] cognitive split between the respected and perhaps loved father of daytime and the very different father of the strange events of the night before. Warned on no account to breathe a word to anyone, including her mother, the child looks to her father for some confirmation of those events and is naturally bewildered when there is no response. Did it really happen or did I dream it? Have I two fathers?' "

The prosecutor waves his hand impatiently. "Spare us the psychological gobbledygook, Mrs. Petersen. Have you, in fact, made any effort to find out what really happened to you? Have you taken a lie-detector test? Have you been hypnotized?"

"Lie detector tests can lie. And hypnosis wouldn't prove anything one way or another either. Some people can't be hypnotized, or they deny under hypnosis events that they really experienced; others are hypnotized and describe experiences that could not have happened. I have put two years of my life into finding out what happened to me. I can't prove it in a court of law, but I know it happened."

The prosecutor raises his eyebrows to signal disbelief. "Surely even the so-called experts would agree that truth is a relative matter. Isn't it presumptuous of you to claim that your version has special validity?"

"He stuck his penis in my mouth."

"Even if that's true, what do you hope to gain by talking about it in public? Aren't you ashamed?"

"I was the victim. He was the one who did something to be ashamed of."

"Are you claiming that there was no pleasure in it for

you?" He holds up his copy of my book and starts turning the pages. "It says right here—"

"I know what it says. My body worked like bodies are meant to work. Nerve endings are nerve endings. Am I supposed to be ashamed of that?"

"Aren't you ashamed of saying so in public? How could you do that to your mother?"

"I didn't do it. *He* did it. He betrayed not only me and my sister, but my mother too. Keeping quiet wouldn't change that."

"But was it really necessary to write so frankly about your mother's drinking? How do you think she's feeling about that right now?"

"Pretty awful, I imagine. She hasn't gotten to the point where she can speak matter-of-factly, or even speak at all, about her drinking. But that doesn't mean I have to collude with her in keeping it quiet. It's part of my story, part of the context of the abuse."

"People will blame her for what happened to you. People always blame the mother. How do you feel about that?"

"My father was the one who abused me, Mr. Prosecutor, not my mother. I don't blame her for what he did. Do you?"

The prosecutor smiles, a thin, cruel smile. He lets the silence build. Then he sighs heavily, as if this is all too much for him to bear. "So you 'had to' tell your story." I hear the quotes around the words. "But did you have to tell it so graphically?"

" 'Incest' and 'sexual abuse' are abstractions which allow people to stay comfortable when they talk about terrible things. That's denial. I wrote about his penis in my mouth because I want my experiences to be real to the reader."

"Why?"

"Because, Mr. Prosecutor, thousands of children and teenagers are being forced to have sex with adults right now, and I want to help create a climate in which they will be supported and listened to."

"If you're so compassionate, Mrs. Petersen, why aren't you concerned about your own children? How are their friends going to behave toward them once this gets out? What kind of mother would even think of exposing them this way?"

"Some of those friends are being sexually abused themselves. In his book *By Silence Betrayed,* John Crewdson cites a 1985 Los Angeles Times poll which surveyed"—I root through my purse and pull out a file card—"two thousand, two hundred and sixty-seven men and women from every state. 'Twenty-two percent of those questioned—twenty-seven percent of the women and sixteen percent of the men—said they had been sexually abused as children.' And that's only the ones who remembered. In my older son's class of fifty-eight teenagers, there could be a dozen boys and girls who have been molested. I know most of those kids, and if that happened to them, or is happening right now, I want them to be able to tell, so it can be stopped."

The prosecutor opens his mouth to reply, but I hold up my hand to forestall him. "What if one of my sons came to me and told me he had been molested? In order to protect himself and other children, he would have to tell police and prosecutors, he would have to face his abuser in court, and he would have to speak much more explicitly than I have in my book. How could I encourage him, or one of his friends, to do such a thing if I refused to do it myself?"

"There are child protection workers, professionals—"

"Who are underpaid and overworked, and even if they weren't, all the professionals in the world can't stop this wickedness if the victims don't use the power that belongs to them. As long as we play by the perpetrators' rules, as long as we abide by the secrecy *they've* imposed on us, we're helpless."

Light from the tall courtroom windows glitters on the prosecutor's steel-rimmed glasses. "I hardly think—"

"The world is full of bigots, Mr. Prosecutor, who will turn on anyone who challenges their bigotry. Is that a reason to keep quiet? Do you think those little first-graders in New Orleans enjoyed being spit on when they walked into that white school? Do you think their parents should have kept them home? And what about the people who helped Jews to escape the Holocaust? It would have been a lot safer for them to sit tight. Do you think we'd all be better off if they'd done nothing?"

The prosecutor throws up his hands, miming disgust. "That was a delightful history lesson, Mrs. Petersen, but I hardly think the jury will see its relevance. I would like to suggest to you, Mrs. Petersen, that this preposterous story you have seen fit to print has not one shred of truth in it, that it is nothing but a tissue of lies from start to finish!"

I meet his eyes. "If it makes you more comfortable to believe that, Mr. Prosecutor . . ."

His face turns a darker shade of purple. "Explain yourself, please."

"Those who feel most threatened by stories about incest are the ones who have been victimized themselves—or who are perpetrators."

"Surely you're not suggesting—"

"If you were molested, you've spent a lifetime keeping it secret, perhaps hoping that it didn't really happen. You have a stake in keeping the lid on any discussion of the subject, as long as you're unwilling to confront your own fears."

Behind his steel-rimmed glasses, white shows around the prosecutor's eyes. *"No!"*

"Most abusers were abused themselves. If you are acting out your history in the present—"

"NO! NO!"

"If you are, you can be helped—but not unless you're willing to look at what happened to you, and what you've done."

I look beyond him to the people packing the courtroom. "I'd like to ask those gathered here today: How many of you are survivors of sexual abuse?"

There is a long silence while people nervously avoid one another's eyes. Then there is a rustle in the back, and a woman stands up: a friend of mine. She is here to support me. I know her story: She was molested by her father, an alcoholic. Another woman stands up, another friend: I know she was molested and tortured by her mother, a pillar of the church. The next person is a man, a stranger. Then another woman stands, and another. Another man, two more women. People are meeting one another's eyes now. Some of them are weeping. Now a woman in the jury box stands up, and then a man. A third of the people in the courtroom are on their feet. The silence continues. Now the judge gets to her feet. I stand too.

The judge clears her throat. "Mr. Prosecutor, do you wish to address the court?"

"Leave me alone!" he cries, his voice high and childish. "Leave me alone!"

"Mr. Prosecutor!" The judge's voice is stern.

"Your honor, I move"—his voice breaks, but he recovers enough to continue—"I move the case against the defendant be dismissed."

KIDS: TWO

I imagine myself getting off the train in Burlingame at the old Southern Pacific depot, crossing the tracks, and walking one block south to Howard Avenue. There is no fog; the sun is shining, casting sharp shadows under the oak and maple trees as I walk past modest houses with tidy front yards, past the big white building where I went to elementary school, past the streets I checked off every day on my way home: Dwight, Stanley, Channing, Bancroft. I used to stop along the way and climb up on tree stumps, looking around to see how the world would look when I was tall. Now I am tall.

Here on the corner of my block is Toby Hecker's house, where we listened to radio programs every night while his mother fixed dinner: *Sergeant Preston, Sky King, The Lone Ranger.* Across the street is Wendy Wheeler's house—her brother Tom taught me to ride a bike. Around the corner lived Helen Rooney, who gave me scarlet fever. And there, across Victoria Road, is the corner park, with the big slide we used to rub with wax paper to make it faster.

Here is my house: 105 Howard Avenue, a cream-colored stucco split-level with brown trim. On one side a path leads back between lush fuchsias, heavy with blossoms that look like ballet dancers. My father's Studebaker stands in the driveway.

I mount the three curved brick steps and approach the front door with its miniature brass grille. I reach out for the handle, depress the latch, and open the door.

I smell the dead ashes in the fireplace and stale smoke from my father's cigars. The sun streams through the Venetian blinds and makes stripes on the Oriental rug. Beside the fireplace, in the big square overstuffed chair, sits the child I was.

She has blond braids and long bangs. She wears brown corduroy overalls and a striped T-shirt, and her feet are bare. I know that the world looks a little bit blurry to this child, because she needs glasses but has not yet told anyone that she can't see.

I walk across the room and touch her on the shoulder. She looks up at me, and I see the marks of tears on her face. I say, "I've come to get you. Do you want to come with me?"

She stretches her arms up toward me, and I reach down and lift her, the shift of weight familiar to me from all the times I've lifted my own children. She is smaller than they were at this age, and I am strong. I lift her easily, and she wraps her arms around me and clings to me. She is safe.

I kiss the top of her head and inhale the clean shampoo smell of her hair. "It's okay," I murmur. "It's okay now."

I call my parents. "Mother? Daddy?" They come in through the open French doors from the backyard, where they have been gardening. My mother is a little smaller than I. Her dark-brown almost straight hair frames her slanting green eyes and delicate nose. My father is tall and strong, much bigger than I, heavy and solid. But I am not afraid. On behalf of the child in my arms, I have courage.

"I'm taking her away with me," I say. "She is not being taken care of here."

My father takes a step forward.

"Get back!" I feel the hair rising on my scalp, my heart beating faster. "Don't you dare touch her! I will never let you touch her again."

The child in my arms clings tighter. She whispers something I don't quite hear. I lean a little closer. "Tell me."

"Do they need me to stay?"

"No. They don't need you. They think they do, but they are wrong. A little girl like you isn't supposed to have to take care of big people like them." My lips are touching her cheek next to her tiny, perfect ear. "You don't belong to them. You belong to yourself now, and you have me to take care of you."

My mother reaches out her arms, and I see the anguish in her face, and remember a winter afternoon I spent playing with my dolls in the dark basement, just through that door on the left. I remember wondering why I didn't feel the affection for my dolls that my friends so clearly felt for theirs. I remember thinking: I'm not ready to be a mother. Will I ever be ready?

Am I ready now to be a mother to this child in my arms? Can I take care of her, protect her, keep her safe? Yes. I am ready now. So when my mother reaches out for her I hold her tighter and say, "You can't have this child. You didn't take care of her." My mother lets her hand drop and steps back.

"Do you want to say goodbye?" I ask the child in my arms.

She turns her face, ever so slightly, in the direction of our parents. "Goodbye," she says in a tiny, muffled voice. I feel her hand on my shoulder lift in a little wave. Then she presses her face against my shoulder and holds tight. She does not look back as we walk to the door.

But I look back. What do I want to say to them? I want to reassure them, to heal my mother's grief. But it is too terrible: They had this child and they didn't take care of her. "I'm sorry this is happening to you," I say. "But I didn't make it happen."

With the child in my arms I make my way carefully down the three brick steps, feeling my way with my foot. On the sidewalk I say to her: "Do you want to walk beside me now?" She nods, and I put her down. I kneel in front of her and gently wipe the tears from her face. Out of the corner of my eye I see my father and mother come out on the porch. I straighten up and take the child's hand. I turn my head and look at them. "Goodbye."

We walk away, the child and I, up Howard Avenue toward the school, the railroad station, and the world.

I sat on the sea-green couch in my therapist's office. Light filled the room, reflected off the bleached wood floor and the cream-colored walls. Kris sat across from me in the big square overstuffed chair. I was talking about how my relationship with my children had changed. "Something is missing," I said. "It's the weight and influence of the past—the anger I dumped on my children that really belongs to my parents. I'm so glad that's gone. But I feel stuck about taking the last step, about letting the feelings of love come in. It's scary. Why is it so scary?"

I started to cry. "Will you come over here and sit next to me?" I asked.

She sat beside me on the couch. "It's being close," she said softly. "You don't know what it's like—that's what's scary."

"If I let myself feel these things, I'll be vulnerable," I said. "The kids will think I'm maudlin; they'll be embarrassed. They'll find me intrusive, find my love intrusive."

I cried harder. She put her arms around me and held me tight. I wanted to be a child in her arms. "I want to put my face against your shoulder," I said. "But I'm afraid I'll get mascara on your blouse."

"If you do, I'll just wash it," she said.

I put my arms around her neck and pressed my face against her.

Though I can no longer lift him, my son Tom at eleven is still young enough to sit on my lap and put his arms around my neck. I love to hold him, to smell his fine, soft, pale hair and kiss his smooth cheek and listen to his laugh.

My son William is thirteen; when he lets me hug him, it's a rare gift to treasure. I have to be ready to let go the moment he's had enough, and wait patiently until the next time.

The way I am with my children has changed since I began to recover my childhood, since I began to recover the child I was when I was abused. The anger is gone, and the driving need to get away, off by myself where nobody can get at me; the need, above all, not to be touched.

I grew up believing I had to do whatever my parents wanted. When I became a mother, I believed I had to do whatever my children wanted. When they called, I went, no matter what I was doing, no matter if I was busy or asleep or sick. "Turn on the water for my shower . . . make me some toast . . . pour me some milk . . . drive me to school . . . take me shopping . . . get me some filler paper . . . get me some ice water . . . turn off my light . . . get me another blanket. . . ." I did it all, most of the time without even asking for a please or thank you. I stopped cooking, reading, writing, even bathing to answer their calls, I stayed up reading to them when I could hardly keep my eyes open, got out of bed in the middle of the night to go to them, even, when I sprained my ankle, crawled up the stairs to them instead of insisting they come down. When they asked me for something, I did everything I could to give it to them. And then I was angry: I was taking care of everybody and nobody was taking care of me.

Learning to take care of myself—to take care of the child I was—has been a slow, painful, terrifying process. When I decided I needed to go to bed at ten o'clock, I had to plan each step, talk about it with my therapist, talk about it with my husband, talk about it with my friends, put on my calendar that on a certain day I was going to tell my children what I had decided, and live through that day up to the point where, ready or not, I took a deep breath, straightened my back, tried to make my voice deep and convincing, and said, "I've decided I need to go to bed at ten o'clock." I didn't feel entitled to sleep when there was anything left to do for anyone.

I said to Kris: "I feel so guilty when they ask me for something and I don't give it to them."

"Notice that guilt," she said. "That guilt means you're changing the way you do things."

After a while the guilt goes away. This afternoon William asked, "Would you make me some toast?"

"Could you make it yourself?" I said. "I'm right in the middle of something." He did, quite cheerfully. Such a small thing, but not to me.

My children get angry with me, as children do, but their

anger is less frightening for me now, and for them. I am beginning to believe that I can survive their anger; and as I grow less fearful, they grow less angry. How terrible it must have been for them when I believed their anger could destroy me.

Now it's possible to set limits; not easy, but possible. My need to protect the child I was gives me courage, as it did in my fantasy, to stand up to those who might be angry with me when I draw the line. The child deserves to be taken care of.

Tom's demands in the grocery store are now a joke we share. "When will you buy me some Jolt cola?" he says, and I answer, "When hell freezes over," and we both laugh.

When I can say no, I can say yes. When I have control, I can give it up and be playful. "You be Monster; I'll be Little Kid," said Tom. I chased him around the house, upstairs and down, growling and stomping my feet while the dogs barked wildly, and I caught him and tickled him and thought to myself: Oh! This is fun! This is what fun feels like!

William and I went to eat lunch in a restaurant with shiny dark walls, neon beer signs, cold air blasting out of the air conditioner, and wonderful smells wafting out from the kitchen. He had spaghetti and meatballs and a Coke; I had a muffaletta and an ice-cold root beer. The muffaletta was perfect, the hot French bread crisp on the outside and soft on the inside, the melted cheese bland, the meat spicy, the olive salad salty and crunchy. We were hungry, we were eating, and we were together.

Another day we drove up and down Lakeshore Drive with the windows open and the radio playing loud. The car filled up with warm air and bright light and music, filled up with time. I had all the time in the world. I didn't want to be anywhere except where I was: driving up and down with my son, flying down the road in a car full of light and air and music and time and love.

GOLD SWORD

The dogs in my dog dreams are the mythic guardians of my personal underworld. They won't let me in until I'm ready to bear what I'll find there; until I'm ready, I won't be able to find my way past them.

I know what happened to me and I am experiencing now the feelings I was afraid to let myself have then. But there is another dimension to memory. I am nearly ready to remember the weight of his body, the dampness of his skin, the smell of cigars on his breath, the way his body hair prickled against me, to remember all that the way I remember the taste of water running out of the garden hose. And I don't want to. I don't want to remember that. I don't want to go to sleep at night: I don't want to be back there in that place. So the dogs protect me. Every night I still wake up, terrified that I haven't fed them and they'll die if I don't.

Is it necessary to remember? My therapist asked me, and I said: Maybe not, not to heal. But it's a spiritual challenge. I've spent my life denying evil, not only my personal evil but the evil all around me: crime, poverty, prejudice, wars, the Holocaust. I managed to see them all as abstractions, without the details that would make them real for me. I wanted to be an island. I didn't want to hear the bell tolling for me.

Now I want to choose. I want to go willingly into that place, terrified but not powerless: like the hero of a children's fantasy. My husband says I need a gold sword.

To confront evil is to see it whole: sight, smell, sound, taste, touch. Not only the facts and feelings but the sensations. And what it means. That a father could do that to his daughter, that my father could do that to me, that he could come to my room in the dark and crawl under the covers with me and press his body up against mine and allow me to press mine against his. That he could put his hand down there, spread open my lips with his fingers, wet his fingers with his spit and later with my own secretions, touch that place I can't bear to name since he named it for me, while I lay still, still, still as a statue, dead as a statue, but feeling those feelings inside, like a point of fire at the center of me. It was my protector, my father, who was doing that to me, and I knew his damp skin his sour smell the softness of his sedentary flesh.

Sometimes he touched me so skillfully that his body and my own seemed to disappear, leaving nothing but a white-hot flame of pleasure below and a pinpoint of consciousness floating far above. But other times I couldn't get away. He put his mouth on mine, his open, huge mouth like a cave; he put his wide, flat tongue as soft as vomit in my mouth; he lapped at my nipples like a thirsty dog. His tongue on my other lips, down there, made me wet and disgusting, as wet and disgusting as his wet disgusting mouth, while I waited alone up above, thinking: Something is happening down below and I won't feel it. His wet tongue, so disgusting, I'm disgusting, it's getting on me, I'll never wash it off, I'm dirty in those awful secret parts of me. I wish I could cut them away, but no, no! How could I cut away a part of my self?

I'm crying now as I write this, rocking back and forth, one hand over my mouth, the other hugging my stomach, trying to hold in the grief and rage. No. I choose not to, I choose to let those feelings out. He can't hurt me anymore. He's dead.

I'm glad he's dead. I wish he had a grave for me to dance on. He wouldn't let me dance, but now I can. I would dance on the waves of the ocean, on the spray of the waves, in the sparkle of my tears as they catch the light, as the shards of his bones caught the light, turning, spinning down toward the water, and the airplane soared above, and I read: "There is a river whose streams make glad the city of God. . . . God is in the midst of her, she shall not be moved." His bones splashed down into the ocean and sank to the bottom, down into the dark where the light will never reach them again, never, never, and salt will dissolve them into dust and they'll never rest on the ocean floor, never rest, but flow and ebb across the miles and miles and miles of the deep, and I'll be dancing on the waves up above.

Someday I'll die too. Before I do I want to tell the truth about him to all the people who think someone like him could never have done something like that. The children whose wounds he mended, the women he dealt with so tenderly and compassionately after he cut their breasts off, the lame and the halt at Crystal Springs. Crystal Springs, the crystal sea, a place in a hymn "where the songs of all the sinless sweep across the crystal sea." But who is sinless? Every single one of us, a devil inside.

Is there something of God in every man, woman, child? In him? If I think of him as a frightened child, the prisoner of his parents, then I can see the light. But he put it out when he crawled into my bed and made me the vessel of his anger.

His hand on mine, holding my fingers on his penis, my arm limp as if I slept, following helplessly the motion of his enclosing hand, up and down, up and down, while he groaned "Faster! Faster!" until it was over. His penis thrusting into my mouth as he stood before me, his long fingers covering my ears, his thumbs pressing too hard against my cheeks, too near my eyes, as he jerked my head up and down. I braced my neck against the motion of his hands, his hair in my mouth, that long thing in my mouth, too big, too big, I'll choke, and then. My mouth full of slime. Too ashamed to spit it out, I swallowed it and gagged. And went to lean over the toilet, wanting to throw up, afraid to throw up, afraid my insides would come out, afraid to let go of the awful slimy secret I had swallowed.

Bastard, bastard, bastard, the bastard of your mother, who loved you as you loved me. Was that little boy's sadness so cold it burned a hole right through your heart? Did you sink into a hole as deep as the center of the earth, far below the shifting dust on the ocean floor? As you died, did you become again a little boy who heard his sister crying when her father did to her the things you did to me? To me and to my sister: generations and generations.

Evil is a little boy crying in the night, a little boy whose mother hates his father and his father hates his mother and his mother loves him, loves him, loves him; he is her one hope, he is all she has, and he doesn't want to be all she has. And he is angry, and he grows up angry, and he tries to be everything everybody ever wanted him to be, and the anger festers, and he comes in the night and crawls into my bed and steals my childhood.

I will get past those dogs when I say: I don't need to wake up and take care of you now, I've taken care of you enough. I can rest, I can sleep, I can remember. The dogs will go to sleep, lying like rugs beside my bed, ready to wake and protect me from the stranger if he should come. If I say to them, "The stranger can't hurt me now," they will let him pass, and I will see him face-to-face. My father's face.

BETSY PETERSEN's articles have appeared in the *Boston Globe*, the *Times-Picayune*, the *Los Angeles Times*, and the *Washington Post*. A graduate of Harvard, she lives with her husband and two teenage sons. *Dancing with Daddy* is her first book.